Belonging and Becoming

Belonging and Becoming

*The Power of Social and Emotional
Learning in High Schools*

Barbara Cervone

Kathleen Cushman

Harvard Education Press
Cambridge, Massachusetts

Library of Congress Control Number 2015937065

Paperback ISBN 978-1-61250-851-1

Library Edition ISBN 978-1-61250-852-8

Published by Harvard Education Press,
an imprint of the Harvard Education Publishing Group

Harvard Education Press
8 Story Street
Cambridge, MA 02138

Cover Design: Wilcox Design
Cover Photo: Nick Whalen
The typefaces used in this book are Minion Pro and Legacy Sans

*For those who daily open the doors
to youth belonging and becoming*

Contents

CHAPTER 1

Integrating Social and Emotional Learning in High School

Key Elements

"A T THIS SCHOOL, they go all out around the student's emotions," Taylor, a twelfth grader, told us. "They ask, they listen. I don't wake up and think, 'Oh I hope this don't happen.' I think, 'I'm OK. I'm fine. I'm ready to learn.'"

At Taylor's South Side Chicago high school, a full-on commitment to social and emotional learning—often referred to simply as SEL—was helping transform the environment from a nightmare of poverty and urban violence to a place where students dream of college.

Two thousand miles away, at Oakland International High School, new English language learners (ELLs) from several continents gathered around tables to critique their drafts of videos about coming into the country. In every classroom, explicit collaborative strategies support their language development, building both community and competency among youth whose prior schooling varies in the extreme.

Both schools are exceptional, to be sure—as are all five of the high schools profiled in this volume. They have turned heads locally and nationally, and they are making all the difference in the world for the youth who depend on them for success. But these schools are not flying solo. Their determination to adopt structures and routines that help students become engaged, responsible, fair-minded, and reflective is part of a small but growing national movement.

We know that standards and accountability, in themselves, do not motivate students to reach high. Research backs up the educator's intuition and experience: students do their best for teachers who show they care. We are learning that character traits like self-regulation, empathy, and "grit" make better students along with better people. Yet developing such qualities rarely figures in the secondary school curriculum. As educators, we are just beginning to wonder and understand how social and emotional growth affects academic outcomes, and why we learn most deeply by enlisting our whole selves.

What structures best nourish strong teacher–student relationships? Can social skills like self-regulation and empathy truly be taught? What most fosters student engagement? And what practices and opportunities can school leaders tap to support those who are ready (or almost ready) to embed SEL into teaching and learning—while continuing to grow the understanding of others who do not yet see the need? How may the strategies vary from school to school, in response to the conditions that make each school unique and shape its climate? What formal and informal measures can schools use to assess the impact of social and emotional learning on student success?

This book, we believe, offers some answers. It also tackles, by intent, the complexities of weaving social and emotional learning into high schools, where curricular coverage and sequence traditionally drive school design and where the need for SEL could not be greater.

SEL AT A CROSSROADS

More than twenty years after Daniel Goleman's landmark book *Emotional Intelligence* indelibly linked thinking and emotions, most public schools continue to value and measure academic competencies as if they bore no relation to social and emotional skills such as self-awareness and persistence.[1] (The former were commonly termed *cognitive* and the latter *noncognitive*, although advances in the science of learning now complicate those terms.) For the first decade of the new century, the overwhelming focus that No Child Left Behind put on literacy, numeracy, and standardized tests consumed much of the oxygen in education policy and practice. Today, the wider and deeper Common Core and other state standards appear to be having, unwittingly or not, a commensurate effect as the focus on content and test prep continues.

Despite the prevailing winds, however, a stream of programs targeting social and emotional learning began to flow into schools across the country starting in the mid-1990s. In turn, a growing body of research attests to the effectiveness of these programs, largely at the elementary grades. In a 2011 meta-analysis of 213 school-based SEL programs, participants demonstrated improved social and emotional skills, attitudes, behavior, and academic performance with an achievement gain of 11 percentile points.[2]

Studies have increasingly shown that factors such as student motivation and engagement, personalization, and student voice improve academic performance. "The movement to raise standards may fail," adolescent development researchers Eric Toshalis and Michael Nakkula concluded, "if teachers are not supported to understand the connections among motivation, engagement, and student voice."[3]

In a 2012 paper on the role of noncognitive factors in adolescent learning, researchers at the Chicago Consortium on School Research (CCSR) identified five critical factors that underpin student success in middle and high school: academic behaviors, academic perseverance, academic mindsets, social skills, and learning strategies. "School performance is a complex phenomenon, shaped by a wide variety of factors intrinsic to students and in their external environment," the authors noted. In addition to content knowledge and academic skills, "students must develop sets of behaviors, skills, attitudes, and strategies that are crucial to academic performance in their classes, but that may not be reflected in their scores on cognitive tests."[4]

In back-to-back commentary pieces in *Education Week* in January 2013, education thought leaders David T. Conley and Mike Rose called, respectively, for rethinking the notions of *noncognitive* and *cognition*. Conley suggested replacing the term *noncognitive* with *metacognitive*: the mind's ability to reflect on how effectively it is handling the learning process as it is doing so.[5] Rose suggested reclaiming the full meaning of cognition—"one that is robust and intellectual, intimately connected to character and social development, and directed toward the creation of a better world."[6]

Meanwhile, few ideas about learning have made their way as quickly into the lexicon of educators as "growth mind-set," a concept based on the malleability of intelligence and introduced by Stanford University psychologist Carol Dweck in 2006.[7] Paul Tough's talk of "grit" in his popular book *How Children Succeed*—based on the pioneering work of University of Pennsylvania researcher Angela Duckworth—has given muscle to the "soft" qualities traditionally attributed to character skills.[8] And long-overdue national attention to the deleterious effects of zero tolerance policies is elevating another strand of SEL: replacing punitive discipline with restorative practices that heal rather than harm.

Educational thinking and practice is at a cusp, we believe, ready to turn away from a dichotomous view of learning and toward a more capacious view that appreciates the complex interplay among academic, social, and emotional skills in the development of adolescent learners.

THE ORIGINS OF THIS BOOK

This volume started as an in-depth investigation of social and emotional learning in U.S. secondary schools. Since 2001, the research arm of our small nonprofit What Kids Can Do (WKCD) had studied, documented, and championed what we call "powerful learning with public purpose" by our nation's adolescents. Although we had never directly examined social and emotional learning, for years we had seen its power: to produce the competent learners our nation seeks and to nourish the responsible and empathic citizens our nation needs. Aware that SEL programs and practices are much more scarce in the higher grades than at the elementary level, we set out to find exemplars that could serve as guides for secondary school educators.

We began our research in 2013 and it continues today. From the start, we were less interested in discrete programs (and their evidence base) than in portraying how schools weave social and emotional learning into their daily fabric. Studying five diverse high schools in depth, we figured, would yield the complex narratives we sought. Our years of documenting adolescent learning had already given us ample opportunity to observe this unique period of tumultuous growth. From test scores, graduation rates, and juvenile incarceration rates, we had seen the results when educators ignore instead of harness the power of social and emotional factors in this developmental stage. Finally, we have long privileged the voices of youth themselves as we document their learning experiences in a form closer to journalism than to academic research. Those interests and biases shape the narratives that follow: portraits of schools at a certain point in their ever-changing histories, rendered through the perspectives of their students, teachers, and school leaders. (In nearly every case, the names of students we describe or quote here have been changed.)

OUR STUDY SCHOOLS

In choosing schools for this study, we looked for schools widely regarded for their excellence in nourishing both the hearts and minds of diverse learners, especially those marginalized by color, class, language, or gender identity. In the schools we sought, adults would have sufficient experience in that work to provide lessons and examples for other educators and school leaders.

As it turned out, four of the five schools we selected had been designed explicitly to link academic, social, and emotional learning. Each was also part of a robust local or national network that shared the same design principles: Expeditionary Learning in the case of Springfield Renaissance School; the Internationals Network for Public Schools in the case of Oakland International High School; the Early College Network in the case of Quest Early College High School; and the New York Performance Standards Consortium in the case of East Side Community School.

The fifth school in our study, Chicago's Fenger High School, offered an extraordinary opportunity to observe educators embracing SEL as a strategy for turning around years of poor performance. At the time of our initial visits, Fenger was in the last year of a three-year federal school improvement grant providing extra personnel and programs tied to SEL.

A CONSTRUCTIVIST APPROACH

In the course of more than fifty combined years of documenting schools that work, we two authors have learned to take a constructivist approach to our research. Rather than bring a list of predetermined issues to the five schools profiled in this book, we worked the other way around. We asked administrators, faculty, and students to show us where social and emotional learning stood out for them in the school day, and what effects it had. We sought information on how they had altered the conventions of "doing school" in terms of time, roles, budget allocations, community involvement, and other areas. The answers varied at each school, in response to the conditions that shaped that school's climate.

We visited each school twice for several days, observing and interviewing as many students and faculty as possible and gathering images and voices for multimedia extensions to our narratives that we posted to our

Web site (see "Resources on the Web"). A year later, in the fall and early winter of 2014, we visited each school again, conducting a new round of interviews to see how their efforts had been sustained and to document how SEL practices were paying off for students in terms of results.

RESOURCES ON THE WEB

As part of our documentation of daily practice in the five schools profiled in this book, we gathered and recorded the voices of students talking about social and emotional learning in various contexts. We also gathered images to accompany their voices. We put the two together in audio slide shows, seeking to bring to life the difference SEL makes in the life of students. Students talk about self-motivation and believing in themselves, opening doors, finding their voice, practicing restorative justice, making connections, and much more.

These audio slide shows can be viewed on our WKCD Web site at www.howyouthlearn.org/SEL_studentvoices.html.

Readers will also find a collection of research summaries, commentaries, stories linked to our five study schools, other short videos containing student voices, and resources for taking action—all linked to social and emotional learning at the secondary level.

SIX KEY ELEMENTS

In summarizing what we saw and heard, we observed six key elements common to our schools that gave social and emotional learning such potency. One comprises structural supports, such as student advisory groups or professional learning teams. Another expands the reach of curriculum and assessment to support the development of SEL competencies. Yet another centers on building an intentional community with shared values, customs, and language; and others concern norms of respect and fairness, or opportunities for students to develop their sense of agency. Each school varied, of course, in how it integrated these elements into its daily work. Writ large, however, the elements themselves stayed constant at all five schools; and school leaders as well as staff directly attributed the success of students to the practices that flowed from them. Exhibit 1.1 summarizes the range of practices, grouped by element, that we found at the schools described here.

Element 1: A Web of Structural Supports

Although none of our study schools enrolled more than six hundred students, their size alone did not ensure that adults would know students well and support their development. A web of structural supports made that possible in these schools.

Daily advisory periods gave every student a home base. Mixed-grade groups of students and a teacher met daily (usually for at least thirty minutes) and often stayed together for four years. Personal discussions, team-building activities, learning and practicing social skills, planning and goal setting—and rarely homework—filled the time, which students at Quest Early College High School called "the heart and soul of this school."

Strong and purposeful student-teacher relationships were the norm. Teachers viewed their role as coaches and facilitators; they kept their doors open, engaged with students in the hallways, and made themselves available before and after school. Again and again, students spoke movingly about how much their teachers cared.

Deliberate structural choices kept class sizes small. Interdisciplinary courses or teaming often decreased the number of students that teachers worked with. East Side Community School chose to offer online language study so as to allocate more teachers for core subjects.

Formal systems for following student progress kept the focus on support, not censure. They included formative assessments and portfolios, along with protocols for helping students the moment they fell behind. Trust replaced shame. "The adults here," a student at Fenger High School said, "they're not going to let you fail, as long as you meet them halfway. They won't let you fail."

Weekly grade-level and subject-area meetings created a professional learning community among faculty. As soon as an issue arose, teachers could consult on students and teaching strategies. Faculty also met regularly as a whole, to learn new practices for helping their students develop academically, socially, and emotionally.

Element 2: An Intentional Community

Research affirms the critical role of shared norms, values, and language in shaping a sense of community in a school and helping students feel they belong. All five schools adopted a mix of traditions, practices, and expectations with the goal of creating a culture that supported and prized the contributions of every member.

Carefully crafted transition programs prepared incoming ninth graders for what they would encounter. Older students typically served as guides. At Oakland International High School, where newly arrived immigrants enrolled throughout the school year, an ongoing "culture of welcome" was especially notable.

Student artwork and posters filled the walls, underscoring behavioral norms. "You'd have to walk around with your eyes closed to not know *exactly* what this school stands for," a Fenger student told us.

Classroom rules, created collaboratively by students and teachers, reinforced expectations. "No matter how many times students hash out class norms," one teacher said, "it always seems to set a tone of community among a fresh group of students."

Frequent rituals and assemblies applauded accomplishments and brought students and faculty together. Procedures were also in place to diffuse tensions that arose in the school community.

Security personnel were regarded as part of the school community. They were trained to de-escalate disruptive behavior. They sought to keep students in school when addressing problems rather than remove them.

Element 3: A Culture of Respect, Participation, and Reflection

A focus on acceptance of differences, inclusive practices, and the habit of reflection added to a sense of belonging and agency among students in each of our study schools. All five schools set 100 percent respect and participation as schoolwide goals, but their strategies for getting there reflected their particular circumstances. For example:

East Side Community School. This school grounded much of its academic coursework in the principles of Facing History and Ourselves, asking students to think through instances of inequity and injustice and consider the choices they make in their own lives. (Since 1976, the Facing History and Ourselves organization has worked with schools worldwide to teach the critical thinking essential to a free society.)

Fenger High School. Here, students learned and practiced a range of social skills in and outside class: asking permission, disagreeing appropriately, having a conversation, making an apology, accepting criticism or compliments, and more.

Oakland International High School. At this school, even newcomers without a word of English found immediate opportunities for expression and participation—not only in soccer and the visual arts but also in the protocols of classroom discussion.

Quest Early College High School. Here, the (two) school rules were clear and simple: respect each other in "creed and deed" and keep the school environment clean and safe. Every aspect of the school's daily operation supported these dicta, including zero tolerance for exclusion and nonparticipation.

Springfield Renaissance School. Students at this school chose the values to which they would be held and then took the lead in reviewing their progress and goals in regular parent–teacher conferences and "passage portfolios."

Element 4: A Commitment to Restorative Practices

Restorative justice serves as a watchword for social and emotional learning, especially in troubled urban schools. Data linking harsh disciplinary policies with dropout rates and, in the case of minority youth, with juvenile detention have ignited a search for constructive alternatives that build trust instead of resentment. We saw robust evidence of these alternatives in the schools profiled in this book. We also saw powerful restorative practices that did not bear that name, meeting students' basic needs for food, shelter, health, and safety.

Peer mediation, peer juries, and peace circles were accepted (and effective) alternatives to detention, suspension, and expulsion. At Fenger, the Peace Room was the heart and soul of the school, and East Side Community made the "public apology" a badge of honor.

Students who arrived at school clearly burdened by circumstances at home could rely on a rapid and empathic response. A quiet room was available for a nap after a night broken by domestic disputes. Students also received a bag of groceries and a stabilization plan when suddenly homeless.

Counseling and therapy groups fostered resilience in the students most at risk. These schools employed on-site mental health professionals; several also partnered with community mental health services or nearby graduate programs in social work.

Programs and practices reached out to families and brought them into school. Parents of Fenger students could request a peace circle to help resolve family conflicts. Staff at most of the schools routinely made home visits. Oakland International integrated family learning and services into the school day.

Element 5: A Curriculum of Connection and Engagement

Student motivation and academic standardization often stand off like rivals, yet our study schools linked engagement and scholarship in ways that mattered to students. Among the many practices we observed:

Serious inquiry required hands and minds at all these schools, and faculty turned often to project-based learning. In learning "expeditions" at Springfield Renaissance, students investigated challenging cross-disciplinary issues, addressing the authentic needs of an audience other than their teachers. Students at Oakland International wrote, recorded, and published their own immigration stories, building impressive skill sets in the process. Advanced statistics students at Fenger conducted an analysis of bullying in the school.

Student choice was a deeply held value that permeated every aspect of these schools. Their students created and monitored personal learning plans; exercised substantial choice among assignments, readings, and topics; demonstrated mastery in different forms and media; and pursued independent projects and extended learning opportunities that built on special interests, culminated in public presentations, and often counted toward graduation requirements.

Reading occurred across the curriculum, steeped in life lessons. These schools explored themes of cultural diversity, identity, dislocation and relocation, and social justice through deep and discursive reading tied to journal writing, reflection, and often independent choice. At East Side, for example, students and teachers started every English class with a half hour of reading anything they chose. Trading books went on schoolwide, and students vied for a place around the table at the principal's regular book club.

Strong evidence of student learning at these schools emerged when students taught each other what they knew. At Quest, students routinely led class discussions and Socratic seminars. In the heterogeneous ELL groups at Oakland International, more proficient students coached and translated for those with less developed English. Students often acted as instructors in East Side afterschool groups such as skateboarding and hip hop beat making.

All of these schools had significant service learning requirements. At Quest, however, every Friday for all four years students left school to volunteer at community sites instead of attending classes. They talked often about the sense of purpose they gained from giving back.

Element 6: A Focus on Developing Student Agency

Each of our study schools trained its sights on students developing the beliefs and habits that result in satisfying and productive lives and learning. Some ways this came across:

Conveying to students that "they matter" and "they can." Schools conveyed this message through encouraging words, caring gestures, invitations to converse, applause for small accomplishments, ready availability, steadfast accountability, and reaching out at unexpected moments.

Encouraging students to find their voice. In class discussions, in personal writing, on issues they cared about, when they felt something was unfair, and when they didn't understand, our study schools encouraged their students.

Helping students push past fear. When learners were trying something new, when they felt exposed (for example, by speaking in public) or apprehensive (for example, when thrust into an unfamiliar role), and when they were confused, our schools were there for their students.

Helping students persist. Our schools also helped students persevere in a subject they believed they could not learn, when they fell far behind and thought they couldn't catch up, when they felt they had practiced enough but were not satisfied with the results, and when distractions exerted a constant pull on their attention.

Inspiring students to grow into something bigger. Our schools inspired students to be the first in their families to go to college, to become mentors to other students, to make a difference in the community, and to turn their own narratives of struggle into stories of agency and resilience.

HOW THIS BOOK IS ORGANIZED

Despite the six elements that characterize all the schools we studied, each has its uniquely interesting story; we organized this volume to bring those narratives to the forefront. With the key elements as a through line, each of the following five chapters describes one school, as observed and profiled by either Barbara Cervone or Kathleen Cushman. Just as the schools themselves have different approaches and styles, so do our separate accounts. However, every chapter includes an introduction to the school's ideas and context, followed by in-depth sections showing the school's particular SEL practices in action. Each chapter closes with a section on how the school has sustained its emphasis on social and emotional learning—sometimes in the face of great odds—and how this emphasis has resulted in improved outcomes for students, especially the student populations for whom success seems so elusive.

Within that frame, these schools' stories reveal differences as well as commonalities. Not unlike personality, a school's culture and climate seem to develop partly from heredity—qualities present from the start—and partly from the pressures of its environment. Recognizing that, we regard our chapters as portraits rather than systematic comparative research. We tried to show the bones each school was born with, which we could see both on the record and in our visits. And yet we also strived to render its character: the kind of sense and sensibility that is incalculable yet unforgettable.

TAKING ACTION

We hope that readers will come away from these five portraits with a new appreciation and understanding of their own school's bones and character. The structures and practices documented here merit close attention from teachers, education leaders, and policy makers alike—whether newcomers or veterans in the world of social and emotional learning. They are powerful demonstrations of what is possible, regardless of whether the practices derive from evidence-based programs or from the thoughtful collaborative work of local schools and stakeholders.

Weaving social and emotional learning into a school's daily life, as these high schools have done, is patient, steady, and painstaking work. It extends much further than adopting, for example, an antibullying program, or adding, say, student advisory groups to the schedule—though both are worthy contributions. Making social and emotional learning core requires a deep commitment from school leadership and staff to do many things differently. Some of those possible actions are big: setting aside one day a week for service learning; turning over several weeks of regular classes to interdisciplinary "expeditions" by students; making time for independent reading for every student, every day. Some are small: a principal's greeting as students enter the building each morning; peace circles as a way to resolve conflicts; classroom norms that prize respectful participation. And many strategies, of course, fall in the middle.

This book is intended for school educators interested in doing things differently, whether their steps are small, medium, or big. But it cherishes the goal of going big: embedding social and emotional learning into a school's overriding formula for student success.

For those setting out to create a new school, the schools profiled here—start-ups themselves, with one exception—offer a multitude of ideas for blending social, emotional, and academic learning in consequential ways. Just as important, their stories chronicle the power of fashioning a school that reflects the particularities of the students it seeks to serve and the communities and circumstances that surround it. Immigrant and refugee youth in Oakland. Working-class students in a New England manufacturing town. African American students scarred by violence on Chicago's South Side. Suburban students outside Houston longing for an alternative to the region's large high schools. Students and families in multiethnic New York City looking to forge community from diversity. The maxim "think globally, act locally" matters as much in school design (or redesign) as it does in other arenas.

This we know for sure: no matter what idiosyncrasies a particular school displays, its intellectual life will inevitably find its heartbeat in the deep social and emotional currents that run through it.

EXHIBIT 1.1   SIX KEY SEL ELEMENTS IN SECONDARY SCHOOL PRACTICE

Elements	Practices
A web of structural supports	• Advisory periods that give every student a home base T • Prioritizing strong and purposeful student-teacher relationships • Design and structural choices that keep class sizes small T • Formal assessment systems that focus on support, not censure • Grade-level and subject area meetings that create a professional learning community among faculty
An intentional community	• Transition programs that prepare incoming students for school norms and culture • Meaningful student expression regarding school norms T • Classroom rules that reinforce expectations, created collaboratively by students and teachers • Rituals and assemblies that bring students and faculty together for recognition and problem solving • Training that makes security personnel part of the school community
A culture of respect, participation, and reflection	T • Opportunities to learn and practice core social skills (e.g., apologizing, decision making, self-regulation) T • Programs and curriculum that encourage substantive dialogue about injustice and civic participation T • Zero tolerance for exclusion and a focus on participation T • Protocols for classroom discussion T • Regular pauses for individual and group reflection
A commitment to restorative practices	T • Prioritizing positive alternatives to detention, suspension, and expulsion T • Rapid and empathetic response to students who are clearly burdened by outside circumstances • Counseling and therapy groups to foster resilience in the most at-risk students • Programs that both reach out to families and bring them into school

EXHIBIT 1.1   *(continued)*

Elements	Practices
A curriculum of connection and engagement	• Project-based learning • Student choice • Reading across the curriculum that connects to life's lessons • Students as teachers • Service learning
A focus on developing student agency	• Conveying to students that "they matter" and "they can" • Encouraging students to find their voice • Helping students push past fear • Pushing students to stretch for something greater

CHAPTER 2

"Belonging, Here and in the World"

East Side Community School New York, New York

IDEA AND CONTEXT

School had only been in session for eleven days on the bright September morning in 2012 when Mark Federman, the principal of East Side Community School (ESCS), got the call from a New York City Department of Education official: "Get everyone out of your building, and get them out fast."

An alert custodian had noticed that the brick facade of the ninety-year-old five-story school building on Manhattan's Lower East Side was pulling away from its steel structure and threatening collapse. Without a moment to prepare, Federman and his staff had to evacuate their 650 students in grades six through twelve, sending them to makeshift shared quarters in widely separated locations.

One year later, that difficult five-month exile had become the stuff of legend in this close-knit school community, whose students reflect the diverse population of its historically immigrant neighborhood. Grades six through eight moved to temporary quarters in another neighborhood school, splintering a staff accustomed to schoolwide collaboration and unity. The high school served its displacement time in a different school—"a school of permanent metal detectors," recalled teacher Joanna Dolgin. Walking into its windowless spaces, "the students had to take off their belts, their shoes, their hair pins, just to come to school. They had to pay a dollar to store their cell phones in a truck. The security guards often were angry with them for not being fast enough."

Students sharply felt the contrast with East Side, where "every casual hallway interaction reminds our kids that they're part of a community, surrounded by adults who support and care about them," Dolgin said. Even the relocated teachers felt isolated and unmoored, she added: "It really reminded me that even the work I do in my classroom is possible because of this larger community that we've created."

When the scattered groups finally returned to their building, everyone seemed to second that emotion. "You can take us out of East Side," reads the message stenciled by the graduating class of 2013 on the wall outside the school's main office, "but you can't take East Side out of us."

Part of a Movement

In the tradition of John Dewey, this school regards community as the prime mover of education in a democracy. Its founding principal, Jill Herman, had in 1985 helped to start Central Park East Secondary School, part of a movement of small, new alternative high schools in New York City during the 1970s and 1980s with roots in the Civil Rights movement and support from local antipoverty nonprofits. As those schools rethought the purpose, structure, and practice of secondary education from the perspective of equity, a national conversation urging high school reform also built momentum, fueled by a series of high-profile reports.[1] By the 1990s, despite a revolving-door series of school chancellors, the New York City Board of Education was developing a national reputation for its "go small" strategy. When in 1992 Herman came from Central Park East to launch East Side Community, the school was one of more than sixty others begun that year in a second wave of the city's small schools of choice.

A decade later, New York's schools came under mayoral control, precipitating a third wave of start-ups under Chancellor Joel Klein. By 2013 small public high schools of choice numbered 136 and had spurred considerable research on their performance. In the aggregate, the data showed that those schools had marked positive effects on the graduation rates of low-income students of color, special education students, and English language learners. A 2013 MDRC report analyzing the twenty-five most effective schools—East Side Community School among them—attributed their success to their combination of academic rigor and personal relationships with students.[2]

A Holistic Approach

Well before the term "social and emotional learning" grew commonplace in the educational lexicon, East Side put all its muscle behind that holistic approach. From the school's start, structures such as advisory groups, portfolio assessment, and community service fostered the social and emotional learning and reflection that buttress academic engagement.

In 2001, when Mark Federman took over from Jill Herman as East Side Community School's principal, he had taught at the school for six years and well knew its foundational values, structures, and practices. Over the next fourteen years, he would focus on developing its strengths further, with collaboration as a primary lever. Where students lagged academically, he supported teachers in far-reaching improvement strategies. He brought the staff together to agree on behavior norms—participation, respect, and restorative action when necessary—that applied to both youth and adults. He adapted the district's teacher evaluation process to cultivate professional growth through collaborative reflection.

"This crumbling building exudes love and care and academic excellence and creativity," one veteran teacher mused, a year after the school joined under one roof again. "It's really hard to be in this space and not get caught up in the fervor of positivity." This chapter illustrates how that came to pass.

THE SCHOOL IN ACTION

Principal Federman inherited an exceptionally stable and committed staff from his predecessor, the school's founder. Teachers were working together to prioritize academic "habits of mind"—emphasizing viewpoint, evidence, relevance, and connection—that took the curriculum deeper for all students. An advisory structure provided two short check-ins daily and two class periods weekly so that teachers could know students well, personally and academically. The school's decision to teach languages as an independent-study elective (with a self-paced software program) allowed it to limit class size to twenty-five students for every teacher. After the launch of a school and neighborhood garden project early on, an ethic of service had spread, with students contributing to and learning from their community. A curriculum partnership with the nonprofit Facing History and Ourselves was introducing ethical dilemmas as a means for youth to evaluate choices both in historical contexts and in their own lives. In a well-developed system of portfolio assessment, students were demonstrating their learning for community audiences.

But the new principal also knew that East Side was struggling with two problems, both familiar stories in urban schools. On the behavioral side, norms and consequences for breaches of conduct varied considerably, undermining the school's avowed culture of mutual respect. On the academic side, students across the grades were reading far below their grade levels. As he took on his leadership role, Mark Federman decided to put those two issues at the center, knowing that they interconnected with every other goal that East Side cherished.

Prioritizing Teacher Collaboration

Federman uses every possible means to distribute school leadership widely and to support collaborative inquiry and initiative among his staff. "The people closest to the students involved always have the most to do with any decision," he said. "They are the experts in their field." Two assistant principals—Tom Mullen for grades nine to twelve and Carla Gonzalez for grades six to eight—serve as instructional coaches for subject areas, as do two veteran teachers and the principal himself.

Daily and yearly schedules at East Side prioritize time for professional learning. In a six-period day, teachers have students in four blocks of roughly fifty-five minutes. Monday through Thursday, another period goes to team planning with subject-area colleagues or teaching partners (such as special educators) and yet another period to individual class prep. On Fridays, students are dismissed at 1:20, giving all staff almost two more hours weekly for collaborative learning.

Before school starts each year, East Side teachers return for a week of collaborative planning. (Their contract requires only two pre-opening days, but Federman says that East Side staff considers the extra time an informal responsibility of "taking part in our professional learning community.") To review and refresh the intentions that result, they meet for two more contractual days for professional development at the end of each semester. The first day goes to a reflective review and assessment of the term just concluded (using survey feedback from students). On the second, grade-level teams look closely at the past term's data from the students they share, identifying areas of concern and setting goals for the semester ahead.

The coherence of the school's academic and social-emotional expectations, Federman noted, results from such regular opportunities for staff from grades six through twelve to meet and "plan backward" from the outcomes they envision. "Throughout the school and across the subject areas, they develop a common language and common practices," he said.

Building Strong Advisory Relationships

The advisory structure at East Side, which rests on common understandings throughout the school community from grades six through twelve, provides a powerful example of this collaborative approach. Teachers here speak often of how student learning in both academic and personal areas increased as they developed shared norms and values through advisory work.

Each advisory group of twelve to fifteen students stays with an adult adviser for a year, then reconfigures. The groups gather for brief check-ins at the start and close of every school day and also meet twice weekly for a full class period. "We're like a tight little family," said teacher Jen McLaughlin. Keeping a close eye on the "temperature" of her advisees as well as their interests, needs, and growing ability to plan and regulate their own lives, she reflected, is "a way of walking through the entire educational and socio-emotional experience with every child."

Although East Side advisers have considerable leeway, they all follow a common framework that emphasizes development in five areas: work habits, mutual respect, health and healthy relationships, the college path, and connections between advisers and their advisees. In addition, the adviser acts as point person for communicating with family, monitoring attendance and academic performance and progress. The adviser's role, as illustrated in Exhibit 2.1, explicitly includes connecting students with extracurricular opportunities and helping them make a productive plan for the summer.

Teachers on a grade-level team often plan together for advisory curriculum and activities across the year. To coach students in positive work habits, eighth-grade advisers developed a series of targeted workshops such as "What's Happening with Your Book Bag?" (on staying organized). Tenth-grade advisers agreed to use advisory time to enable students to collect samples from city waterways for a chemistry portfolio project.

All five strands of the advisory curriculum help students "know that there's somewhere for them to be able to express their feelings," said Gonzalez, the assistant principal for the middle grades.

"We're teaching them how to advocate for themselves, not only in healthy relationships but also in their work habits. We're letting them know that they have a voice within the community—that if you speak up, somebody will help you, advocate for you. It really makes a difference in how they're carrying themselves throughout life in our school—in terms of self-esteem, respect for themselves, and knowing what they have a right to."

For example, Amber Joseph, a learning specialist who supports English and social studies classes, started her eighth-grade advisees' year with a project exploring their own identities. As they looked ahead to the high school transition, it helped allay their anxiety about what peers thought of them, she said.

"They made two boxes: what you think about yourself, and what you think other people think about you. When we discussed it, they realized that a lot of what they think about themselves is totally different than what other kids think about them. And it's actually positive. Like kids were writing, 'I think other people think I'm shy' or 'Other people think I don't have a lot to say.' And other students were like, 'What?! You talk all the time!' So it's just for them to think about perception. And a good exercise, too, for teachers—'cause we do that with them, too."

In the spring, as many students in her group were dealing with their first relationships, Joseph asked them to brainstorm what makes a relationship "good" or "healthy." Again she did the exercise along with them, sharing some of her own expectations and boundaries regarding her mother, her best friend, and her roommate. "Why might you have different expectations depending on the people?" she asked her students. "Are there any expectations that all your relationships have in common?"

Five times yearly, parents and guardians join in a three-way conference with student and adviser to review progress and revisit goals. Advisers use e-mail and text messaging to keep families in the loop about out-of-school opportunities as well. "There's always someone who's willing to speak with my parents in Spanish and take their time to explain things," said Brandon. "That sends a huge message to my parents." Jason, who divides his home life between parents, said simply, "This is somewhere that my family feels comfortable. It's a really nice environment that you always wanna come back to."

Such conversations also support college planning in families with little experience in that area. Research shows that students talk and listen more to their teachers about postsecondary planning than they do to counseling staff,[3] and East Side advisers engage in that dialogue from middle through high school. Starting as early as sixth grade, advisories visit college campuses to increase awareness of what opportunities lie ahead.

Committing to 100 Percent Respect

The mutual understanding developed in advisory provides a foundation for the overarching East Side behavior norm known as "100 percent respect." Far more than a slogan in this school, this policy guides an active commitment to trust, openness, and mutual support among youth and adults in the common enterprise of learning.

Matthew Guldin, a former dean of students who developed the approach, saw it as a fundamental shift in school culture that would take root over years of concentrated effort.[4] In 2005, in a democratic process, groups of teachers, staff, and students first identified behaviors that signaled the respect they hoped to receive as well as behaviors they could not countenance (see Exhibit 2.2). Then they agreed on routines and activities—such as mediation and the public apology—by which anyone at the school would acknowledge harm done to others and make appropriate amends, without humiliation. Each year, East Side advisories revisit those behaviors and agreements to keep them current, check for understanding, and bring newcomers into consensus on the compact.

When the teachers model such an apology in class, said Luis Rosado, the school's dean of students, "it's simple and easy. It's important for the kids to see that. Then if it ends up being their turn, they know not to make a big deal out of it.

"The teacher would say, you know, 'I made a mistake 'cause I threatened everybody with detention when it was only a few people who were out of line.' And the kids'll be like, 'Oh.' And then the teacher'll move on: 'My mistake. I apologize. I shouldn't have spoken that way.'"

If a student has great anxiety about speaking in front of others, a letter of apology and a private conversation may suffice. But over time, students learn to express their regret publicly to the group, said Chris Osorio, the assistant dean for the middle school and also its basketball coach.

"It's something sincere and genuine like, 'I was completely wrong on Monday when I walked in twenty minutes late. It was inappropriate of me. I shouldn't have done that. And then when I came in, I definitely disrupted the lesson. Interrupted your education. I let you guys down. I let the teachers down. And I understand what I did and I'm gonna do my best to correct it.' Something to that effect, where they take ownership over it."

When a student violates the shared norms of respect, "the teachers are definitely our first line," Rosado said. "They don't just say, 'This is a problem kid. I want him out.' They will work with the student. They'll usually identify things before it blows up, and that's important." In formal and informal ways, "we try to give the students the opportunity to speak," he added.

"A lot of these kids, they have emotional concerns that would stop them from coming to school if they didn't have that opportunity to vent. It's important that they know they can rely on everyone they see. So any educator in the building has multiple hats that we fit—nurse, counselor, teacher, mentor, coach. Whatever the kid needs, we try to provide it to them."

When it comes to where students can turn for social and emotional support, this school builds in redundancy. In addition to its dean of students and a school psychologist, East Side has assistant deans at the middle and high school level, a guidance counselor, and a social worker, along with graduate interns in social work from a nearby university who volunteer several days a week. "We're huge on being preventive," said Osorio. "We tell the kids it's a lot easier to sit down and speak one-on-one than it is to try to confront a teacher in front of a classroom. That's never gonna work for you—and the same way with us."

Joe Hill, the assistant dean for the high school, has spent more than a decade at East Side and now also serves as assistant to the principal. "When you say 'trouble,' it could be both positive and negative, in a good way or a bad way," he said, with a laugh.

"[Behavior] incidents provide a good teaching moment, for the child and yourself. Let them know that you can grow from this. You can learn from this. Reflect on it and, you know, if it happens again, we'll ante up a little bit. But mistakes are gonna be made as you grow."

For Crystal, a student who had experienced her fair share of conflict with peers, that attitude had a calming effect. "Since I came here, I get in less trouble," she said. "Most teachers treat us like their own children. They're coming from their heart saying how they feel and what they want you to do to be a better person."

Exploring Choices Through History

The cultivation of respectful practices in a very diverse community resonates deeply with the principles of Facing History and Ourselves, a curriculum partnership that has influenced the culture at East Side since the early years of the school. Its framework, rooted in historical instances of inequity and injustice, focuses on the very questions of belonging, identity, and agency that research suggests most affect the academic engagement and the social and emotional resiliency of adolescent learners.[5]

First used in a tenth-grade history course at East Side, the approach resonated with the school's founding philosophy of "community taking responsibility for community," Mark Federman said. Soon other history teachers and then advisory groups began to integrate its themes as teachers and students engaged with academic work and with each other.

Danny Lora, who teaches global history to ninth graders, now starts the year with a unit about identity and culture. "Students themselves spoke about moments when they were labeled, moments when they felt like outcasts, when they felt like they didn't belong," he said. "And then it came full circle to the history that we study," in subsequent units on world religions and the Israeli–Palestinian conflict.

"It all connects to belonging—here, and in the world, period," said Sarima in the spring of her senior year. East Side "opened my eyes to a lot of things," she reflected. "Stereotypes that go around, and things in the world that I would've never learned.

"What it means to be you. Like some people might see you and think, 'Oh, you're this and that.' And you're like, 'No. Actually I'm this and that.'

But they're like, 'But you don't look like that.' You're like, 'But it's what I want to identify myself with. Therefore I *am* it.'"

The Facing History framework also fosters the understanding that different choices can result in different outcomes. As students like Sarima think and talk about inclusion and exclusion, obedience and resistance, they often recognize similar patterns in their own lives and choose to act in new ways.

"We're all capable of prejudging somebody based on their skin color, their gender, whatever," said Fakhira, a twelfth grader who described her younger self as "the class clown always getting kicked out of class for making some joke." Her tenth-grade global history class, which explores the Holocaust and other historical clashes of values, made her rethink her biases and also her behavior, she reflected. "You really get to see how society does have an effect on you."

"There's this long-term ripple effect that happens with students, I think," said Yolanda Betances, who teaches that class. "It's a sense of building community, working as a community, helping students to consider topics from other people's perspectives, even in advisory. It's about values, it's about character developing, it's about them thinking about how they make decisions, not only in the now but later on in life."

By senior year, for example, Fakhira was applying her insights about prejudice in a research paper on the sociology of education that would be part of her graduation portfolio. The U.S. education system, she argued, generally "limits the access to opportunity and emulates a criminal and prisoner atmosphere" for poor and minority students. She portrayed her own school, in contrast, as "a place of opportunity" that supports students in developing both identity and agency as they discuss "issues that have affected the world such as slavery, civil rights, [and] apartheid as well as issues that are currently affecting the world such as abortion, gun control, and women's rights."

A classmate, Nakhal, called on postcolonial theory in writing a paper that analyzed identity, subjectivity, and power in casual language usage. "Throughout the day I listen to people of color call each other 'my n***a,'" she wrote. "This N word seems to be passed around a lot with no emotion," she continued, conjecturing that it conveyed the speaker's attitude, "No, you don't have power to put us down." But because the term's original intention was "to downgrade people like myself," Nakhal concluded, "the way to resist oppression is to stop using the word."

Considerable scaffolding throughout the high school years goes into the scholarship that students display in such work. With her eleventh graders, for example, Joanna Dolgin uses texts like the graphic novel *Persepolis* to explore the power of societal norms. In one assignment "we had to break a norm," her student Erick said. "You know how on public transportation, if it's empty you don't sit next to somebody? Well, I tried to sit next to somebody, and you could definitely tell that they were frustrated. But we also looked at why people *don't* get frustrated if the bus is packed and you sit next to them."

As students grow more aware of how social norms work, they also develop a sense of agency in choosing whether to uphold or ignore them. "I realized that I actually go along with social norms sometimes, even though I don't notice it," Amber said. (She gave "Don't snitch" as an example.) But even norms that are common elsewhere frequently shift at East Side. "It's the norm *not* to cheat," Amber noted. "Because the school expects better from its students." (In any case, East Side's academic culture of collaborative inquiry and performance assessment largely renders cheating a moot point. Students are expected to contribute to each other's class work, and they individually present and defend their work to outsiders in high-stakes roundtable presentations.)

The sense of responsibility to the local community—a founding principle of the school—permeates many academic activities here. Around the lab stations in Joseph Vincente's chemistry class, tenth graders clustered to test the quality of water from the nearby East River. After they grasped the concepts underlying treatment of contaminated water, "we'll look at things from an environmental, economic, social equity standpoint," their teacher explained. "The water treatment plant on 14th Street, how is that different and similar to this? How would you do it in a poorer community that doesn't have access to clean water already?" To demonstrate their learning, students would create short video public-service announcements on different water quality issues and present them to East Side sixth graders. If someday students could "go to the voting booth and make smart decisions, based on science," Vincente said, his class would have met its key goal.

Belonging in Academic Inquiry

From their first day at East Side Community School—in advisory groups, in classes, in the lunchroom, in their elective activities, and even their free time—students begin to engage in hard conversations about issues that have no easy answers. Why do more girls apply to college than boys? Should the school cafeteria supply flavored milk despite the empty calories it holds? Does telling someone to "man up" constitute offensive stereotyping? Can the arts be used to oppress, not just to express? Can a military campaign justify violence against civilians? Starting with matters that directly connect to their lives, they examine the effects of personal choices in both the private and the public sphere.

The teenage years are ideal for students to train their minds on matters with social resonance, research shows.[6] As adolescent learners explore new perspectives, analyze evidence, and come to their own decisions, they are not just learning academic skills but also shaping an identity: a sense of who they are and who they want to become.

Teachers at East Side attune their lessons to that ongoing social and emotional development. After Kathleen Schechter asked her eighth graders to act out *Twelve Angry Men* in class, for example, she had them compare the personalities of different jurors to those of their classmates. "It reminds me of fights with my friends, when we're trying to decide something," said Alyssa.

In fact, Schechter had chosen the play with the goal of opening minds. "A lot of these students are young men and women of color," she noted. "Not only are people going to stereotype them, but they stereotype one another." If taken up earlier in the year, she said, the same literary text might have daunted her students with its sophisticated themes and vocabulary. "But by the spring they're more like high school students, more aware of what's going on in their neighborhoods and the world around them. I like them to know their rights."

Whatever the academic domain, from the middle grades through high school, East Side students get continual practice developing their own ideas, considering those of others, and revising their thinking with the benefit of critique.

"They learn how to talk to each other, how to listen, how to be respectful, how to draw on their own lives and analyze the world around them," said English teacher Joanna Dolgin. Yet rather than "just sit here and talk about feelings," she emphasized, students must support their positions, both in speaking and in writing. "They need to read complex and difficult texts and make sense of them and not give up."

"We want them to see that their efforts are increasing their intellectual ability and competence," said Ben Wides, who teaches history to twelfth graders. "So we're very deliberate about teaching skills that will help students work more independently."

When her tenth graders have trouble engaging with a task, Yolanda Betances noted, her priority is to "know what's going on with them." As her class read through a difficult text, she moved to those who seemed adrift and checked their understanding. "Can you read that over again?" she said quietly to one student. "What do you think that says?"

Students recognize the classroom scaffolding that supports them in serious inquiry. "You have to be confident that you won't be criticized for your opinion," said Makayla, crediting her literature teacher, Kim Kelly, for creating "a safe place" for disagreement. "She doesn't allow people to call people's ideas stupid or completely disregard your opinion." On the other side, listening to critique without getting defensive also takes practice, she noted. "You have to understand that it's your opinion that they're attacking, not you."

"But we've also learned how to defend," her classmate Rafaela put in. "Because it's not enough to just state your opinion—we also have to provide evidence. Where do you see that happening? At what point in the book did your opinion change and make you stand on where you stand right now?" That habit of mind serves her well, she added. "You move what you learn from this class to other classes."

"They start to anticipate that need to support their perspective," Wides agreed. "And I think it does increase their confidence. They have a sense that, you know, 'I'm learning to do pretty sophisticated stuff.'"

For a young man named Derek, the sense of belonging in an academic activity has increased his willingness to work hard at it. "I don't feel like I'm lower than the adults; I feel like I'm treated the same way as they are," he said. "You're showing that you wanna be on that team. You wanna help everybody else succeed, and you wanna succeed with them."

Fakhira had always found science difficult, but in senior year the desire to work alongside her peers won out over her reluctance. "I've learned the discipline from this girl right here," she said, pointing to her best friend, Sarima. "And when I became friends with her, all my other friends pushed me to be more."

"We never quit on a student," Jen McLaughlin declared. "Even the kids that aren't struggling, they see what happens with their classmates who don't have things as easy. They all pull together and help each other. They all want to cross the finish line together. And it's extraordinary what happens."

Building a Schoolwide Culture of Reading

East Side's communitywide commitment to building a culture of reading provided the rock-solid foundation on which such ambitious work took place. It began in the early 2000s, principal Mark Federman recalled, when he recognized that "most students would not—and many could not—read the texts in front of them."[7] Students clearly viewed reading as a chore, not as a pleasure or even a resource.

Federman and his faculty set out to transform that attitude using three key strategies:

1. They would give all students easy access to books they wanted to, and could, read.
2. They would ensure uninterrupted, uncompromised time to read those books independently and at home.
3. They would coach and model how to choose books, plan for reading, and practice the habits powerful readers use when they interact with text.

Ten years later, East Side Community School had the lively and inviting aspect of a small-town book fair. Not just the well-stocked school library but every English language arts classroom was bursting with books at every reading level, in milk crates labeled "Teen Fiction" or "Horror" or "Sports." Placards on classroom doors advertised what the teacher inside was reading for pleasure, and teachers had funds to replenish their classroom libraries with books they thought would appeal to particular students. Nothing empowers a young reader more, Federman believes, than having an adult walk up with a book and say, "I saw this book, thought of you, and bought it for my library so you could read it." Kids routinely stopped by his office to browse his own handpicked library of two thousand titles, and they vied to participate in his Principal's Book Club discussions (complete with pizza).

The freedom to choose what they read built both value and confidence for students like Christian, who said he previously had "viewed reading as a punishment." Now, when teachers assigned more difficult texts, he said, "because I've read all these other books, I think in my mind that I'm capable of finishing this book." Even his very reluctant peers eventually got on board, he observed. "There's so many different people in the school reading, and everybody's pressuring them, 'Oh read this book, read this book, this is interesting, read that.'"

The East Side school schedule sets aside twenty to thirty minutes for uninterrupted, nonnegotiable independent reading by students and teachers at the beginning of all English classes—sufficient quiet time, as Federman said, "to fall in love with reading and get lost in books." Another hour of nightly independent reading is also expected (and documented). Teachers have regular reading conferences with individual students, helping them make independent reading choices that suit not only their interests but also their needs. And students maintain a "goal list" of books they want to read, in order of increasing difficulty. Because they are stretching for something they desire, Federman says, they are much more likely to reach it.

The robust community of reading that now permeates East Side's school culture was built on a fundamentally social and emotional platform. Its teachers developed their strategies together as a community of practice, sharing their own reading experiences as well as their ideas for helping students read better. They had the time and support to do so, including funds for books, an expert literacy coach, and professional development opportunities. The change itself was nonnegotiable—East Side students were going to become independent readers—but teachers made it happen together in their own chosen, individual, negotiated ways, just as their students would later begin to do. And the academic results were dramatic: standardized reading assessments showed students' skills leaping ahead at a rate two to three times that of their peers nationwide.[8]

Equally important, Federman noted, independent reading provides support to adolescents who might otherwise struggle in isolation with social and emotional issues such as homophobia, bullying, sexual relationships, or abuse. The many excellent young-adult books on such difficult topics make it far easier to open thoughtful youth–adult conversations on such topics—"bibliotherapy," as he calls it.

"Instead of a punishment, now I view it as an escape in a way," Christian affirmed. "If anything is going wrong, if I have any problems, if I feel down, if I pick up a book and I start to read, those minutes are a whole 'nother world. It helps me cope with the things that I'm coping with."

Taking Creative Expression Seriously

East Side regards creative expression as part of its core curriculum, with two full-time visual art teachers and a number of part-time instructors in dance, music, and other arts. By enlisting teaching artists from the community, the East Side schedule manages to offer elective choices including not just visual arts and media but also dance, cooking, creative writing, beat making and beat rhyming, rock band, choir, and chess.

Many students described the expressive arts as the space where they felt most free to be themselves. "Dancing is making a story with your body, expressing yourself in different ways," said a girl who had been practicing dance moves with a group on the stage in the school auditorium. "You can't do that in all your classes." Her choice of dance class also allowed her to exercise autonomy in accumulating credits toward graduation: it counted toward the district's physical education requirement.

In numerous ways, making art also supports social development. Ian, a ninth-grade boy, described honing his collaborative skills in his class in rock music. "We work together as a team. When we do the songs, we have to have a close bond with each other—eye contact, communication—so that we won't mess up. We kind of hop it up so that everyone can be in tune with us as well, and we all help each other with that."

The visual arts offer a way of thinking that transcends traditional academic skills, noted Leigh Klonsky, who teaches digital arts and media. Young people experience continual pressure to think, speak, and write well, she said, but "it's very hard and different to think and express yourself visually." Students keep a daily art journal in class, sketching out their ideas and practicing artistic techniques.

"Things come up visually that verbally you're not able to communicate, and so they have not been noticed in other classes," noted Desiree Borrero, the visual artist who coordinates the East Side art program. "The arts give an emotional outlet to kids." For one student painter in a period of distress, she recalled, art class provided the sole motivation to come to school. That same young man now attends a highly regarded New York City college of art, on full scholarship.

"Understanding your world in a visual way completely affects your feeling of self-worth and confidence as a whole person," declared Klonsky. "I know I felt it as a kid in Chicago public schools, not having it until I was in high school." Partly for that reason, both art teachers devote substantial time to making public the work of East Side students. They persuaded the school to allocate space for a large gallery on the building's lower level, and each year they mount several shows, displaying and selling student artwork alongside that of teachers and local artists. The practice "gives them another possibility in their lives," said Borrero. At least one East Side graduate each year goes on to study art, she noted with satisfaction, and some have made it to very selective institutions.

Learning Outside the Classroom

Extracurricular activities are as important as classes here—for balance, for academic enrichment, and because they give students chances to develop their identities and relationships. Like parents who seek every advantage for their children, teachers and staff at East Side are always looking to create substantive and lasting learning from whatever most excites their charges. Although the school does not require staff to sponsor afterschool groups, many gladly choose to take that role.

Every Tuesday after school, science teacher Erica Ring meets with her afterschool environmental committee, a rotating group of twenty to thirty students in grades six through twelve who work on the school's recycling and energy reduction efforts and also manage a large garden on school grounds. On one early spring day, a cluster of youth was choosing what species to plant in order to draw hummingbirds to the garden.

"I love these weeks of planning and planting," Ring said, "because these are the times when I say the least. The students have totally taken over." The project not only builds students' organizational skills, she noted, but also requires enough physical effort that she may propose it be granted a P.E. credit. "I've never seen them work as hard," she noted. "Turning a load of compost takes about forty-five minutes of full-out sweat."

A recent grant from the Pollination Project kept students at work during the summer months, creating rodent-proof raised planting beds for use by East Side and the surrounding community. Ring envisions the garden developing into a year-round service project, complete with interns, a gardening class, and the opportunity for students to earn certificates as "junior master gardeners."

East Side adults go all out to know what makes students tick—even those who appear alienated from academic pursuits. A twelfth grader known as J. J., who hoped for a career in music, assembled a small music studio at home. "Why do I need to learn how to figure out the area below a parabola?" he asked, defending the time he devoted to it. "I could work all night on a song, but I can't do that with schoolwork."

Yet when his precalculus class learned about sine waves, J. J.'s music experiences helped him understand its relevance immediately. He was also using his technical knowledge to assist other students in a beat-rhyming class led by a teacher he admired. "We talk about life, philosophy, and stuff," he said. "So I come to the class, show support, talk about things."

When students seem socially disconnected in some way, teachers seek to broaden their horizons. Jen McLaughlin worried aloud about an English language learner who was driving himself hard academically while avoiding clubs or other activities. "I want to try and find something for him to do in the school to get him more hooked in to the school community," she said. "I want him to feel like he really fits and belongs here, too."

Sarima, who worked relentlessly for high grades, said that her ninth-grade English teacher, Dipa Shah, first encouraged her to create a healthier balance by joining student government. "I'm not an athlete, I'm not a dancer," she said, but she found that group exciting and by senior year served as its president. "Outside of school work, you have something else to look towards," she said with satisfaction.

Extracurricular learning also stretches students to think about their identities and aspirations. A group of girls and two women teachers began a lunch club called Sisterhood to explore the pressures of being female in a culture filled with stereotypes. Over salad and soup one day, they first analyzed a series of highly sexualized media advertisements and then moved on to a lively discussion of the merits of East Side's dress code.

When Natalie was in seventh grade at East Side, a teacher recommended a math enrichment activity after school. Now a senior, she plans to study electrical engineering in college. "I could have gone another path," she said. "But the teachers here actually help you and are involved in your life as well. I was supported throughout all my years here, and I decided to keep moving forward and pursue my goals."

A sixth grader named Mia had recently learned chess, offered here as both an elective and a club. "I feel so free when I'm playing chess," she said, across the table from her chess partner in a small room filled with other pairs intent on their play. "Because nobody can tell me where to move or what to do. And I get better by doing tactics. It just makes me feel good. It's what I'm good at."

Every day in advisory, students and advisers comb through a bulletin from the counseling office that lists new possibilities. "Our responsibility is to help make sure that they're doing something productive over the summer, and that they're involved in afterschool activities that match their passions and their needs," said Carla Gonzalez, the assistant principal for middle school.

"Whatever it takes," agreed the high school assistant principal, Tom Mullen. "When you know students well, you can start tailoring programs that will meet their needs and tap their interests." For example, Leigh Klonsky has helped many of her art students enroll in outside classes at New York University and the Fashion Institute of Technology. With her colleague Desiree Borrero, she also helps organize annual group trips abroad for students who otherwise might never leave the city.

Borrero recalled a girl who—after hundreds of hours spent preparing for their first trip to Europe—decided to back out. "They had done 180 hours of service, including fundraising. They took afterschool art courses and language classes. We even went out and tried different foods that they'd be eating," she said. "Most of the kids had never left New York City, ever. And I think she started getting scared." A few weeks later, looking out over the hills of Assisi, the same student told her, "This is why you didn't let me quit." In that student's four years of college, the teacher added with pride, "she has now gone to three different countries and helped build communities as well. She wrote me, 'When this all started, I never knew that traveling would be part of my life like this.'"

Wherever he goes and whomever he meets, Mullen keeps a sharp eye out for potential community partners and seeks grants to bring them in. Funds raised by the school's parent association or the nonprofit Friends of

East Side pay for some activities; a partnership with Beacon, an initiative of the city's Department of Youth and Community Development, makes others possible. East Side students can choose from at least fifty such activities, including a skateboarding program, several bands that practice in the school basement, a choir, two hip hop groups, a dance group, a weekend photography program, a bicycling group that takes on a 100-kilometer challenge, and a rock-climbing and mentorship program at a Brooklyn gym.

Mullen sees a contagious confidence develop as young people stretch for something they once regarded as beyond their reach. "They realize, 'You know what? I can do things,'" he said. "That leads to confidence in the classroom. And it pays off."

RESULTS AND SUSTAINABILITY

Since its start in 1992, East Side has steadily built a reputation in the district and beyond as a student-centered middle and high school where both youth and teachers thrive. In surveys collected in 2014 from parents and students for the district's annual "school quality snapshot," students overwhelmingly attested to their safety on the premises and their interest in school programs, classes, and activities; parents and teachers also expressed near total satisfaction.

From 2006 to 2014, the era in which the New York City Department of Education gave schools annual letter grades on their progress and performance, both the middle and the high school at East Side received an A each year. The school's high school graduation rate was 15 to 20 percent higher than the city average, with 81 percent of its 2014 class graduating within four years (compared to two-thirds for the city as a whole).

Mark Federman calls East Side "a true progressive school," because it commits to continual social, emotional, and academic development. "We're all about making progress," he said, "in the community, and as a community." Accountability at East Side necessarily marries with that sense of community. At every level—personal behaviors, academic performance, professional advancement, even state oversight requirements—this school evaluates and decides important matters in ways that respect the judgment of those closest to the situation.

Making Learning Public

As evidence of student proficiency, East Side follows a very different public accountability procedure than do most New York City high schools. The school belongs to the New York Performance Standards Consortium, which in 1997 won approval from state education authorities for twenty-eight high schools to substitute high-quality portfolio assessments for all but one of the five Regents exams required for graduation. Consortium membership now stands at forty-eight, after other like-minded schools made their cases to join the group in 2013.

Membership in the Consortium has included East Side in a trove of aggregated research data on its educational outcomes overall.[9] Although students enter Consortium schools with lower average scores for English language arts and math than citywide averages, they significantly outperform students in other New York City public schools. Serving a similar population and following the same admissions process as other nonexam district schools, Consortium schools show half the city's dropout rate, and their graduation rates for English language learners and students with disabilities are nearly double. On other indicators, Consortium students have fewer discipline issues. Suspensions are 5 percent, compared to 11 percent for New York City high schools and 12 percent for city charter schools. Consortium classrooms also maintain far greater teacher stability than the city average. Turnover rates are 15 percent for Consortium schools, 25 percent for charters, and a staggering 58 percent for New York City high schools overall.

East Side's performance-based assessment practices afford a robust method of validating its academic standards and student outcomes within the larger community of Consortium partners. They have also shaped the school's curriculum and instruction in deep and far-reaching ways, which call into play many of the key elements set forth in our introduction.

At the end of every semester, when students in most New York City high schools are taking the state Regents exams, their East Side peers instead present and defend their work at roundtables for teachers and outside evaluators. Students write an analytical essay on a piece of literature for English and an argumentative social studies research paper. They conduct or extend a science experiment and demonstrate problem solving at higher levels of mathematics. And in all areas, students are also required to defend their work orally as well as through written products. Evaluations using rubrics like that in Exhibit 2.3 by at least two teachers at the students' school as well as an outside visitor ensure the reliability and validity of the process.

In his welcome memo to roundtable visitors, Mark Federman describes the high stakes involved:

> We—meaning the students, staff and school as a whole—will put it all out there for each other, our families, our friends, our colleagues and our community to see: the good, the bad, and everything else. This is not an easy thing to do. Our students' work and our own work is not always as pretty as we want it to be. And no matter how hard they have worked and we have worked, we are never quite satisfied. However, we offer it to the public because it is to the public that we and our students are ultimately accountable.

The regularity of these twice-yearly rituals—six in each core subject by the time they reach senior year—means that East Side students get continual practice in oral and written reflection on their own work and in answering questions about the work from the larger community. For presentations by ninth through eleventh graders, each visitor sits with two students in a room where simultaneous roundtables are taking place. The graduation portfolio required in the senior year includes a major research paper. Its presentation resembles a dissertation defense: a private session with two or three adults who have prior access to the work and enter into deeper discussion and feedback.

To succeed at this kind of assessment, students also must work over time on skills such as planning, persistence, and communication. "In some ways it's kinda stressful," Josh reflected in twelfth grade.

"Because you have different classes and you have different deadlines, and you've gotta meet those deadlines. And it's a lot of work as far as preparation for the presentation. But once you get up there and you're doing your thing, it's like you're the teacher and they're the students. It's that whole transition; you feel good about yourself afterwards. And then when they write that 'excellent' or that 'pass' on your profile, it's like an overwhelming feeling of greatness in you."

"I cannot possibly explain how enjoyable and impressive it was to listen to the students," wrote guest evaluator Steven Lazar, a National Board Certified social studies and English teacher with long experience in New York City public high schools, who brought his teaching colleagues to a day of roundtables in 2011. He added:

> Particularly in the senior class, the standards for students were higher than any school I have ever encountered. Students were not only doing high-level college literary analysis, but they displayed an amount of reflection, self-awareness, and thoughtfulness that most adults do not have. . . . We saw the value of having students formally reflect on their learning. We saw how much more impressive students' understanding and complexity of thought is when they have the opportunity to go in-depth over a smaller amount of skills and content, rather than emphasizing a limited understanding of a breadth of content. And we saw that students are capable of much, much more than what is tested on the state's exams.[10]

Students' ideas often approach serious scholarship, said history teacher Ben Wides, by the time that twelfth graders must choose a topic for the culminating research paper in the graduation portfolio. Sometimes they pick an issue of personal interest, but he feels even greater satisfaction when he sees students "learning for learning's sake—looking at a real question, engaging in intellectual inquiry on a topic that does not relate personally to them. That's the essence. And the fact that they're constructing it for themselves, I think, is really powerful."

Becoming College Ready

Strong evidence of the predictive validity of the school's graduation assessments comes from the research on overall postsecondary outcomes of students in the Performance Standards Consortium. In 2011, 86 percent of African American and 90 percent of Latino male graduates of Consortium schools were accepted to college. (National averages are 37 percent and 43 percent, respectively.) Ninety-three percent of Consortium graduates remain enrolled in four-year colleges after the first two years, compared with an average of 81 percent nationally. Yet Consortium students are far more likely to be low income than the U.S. average.

East Side Community School provides a look at how those positive outcomes develop. The staff works closely with students on postsecondary planning, starting as early as grade six. A key partnership with College Bound Initiative (an initiative of the Young Women's Leadership Network) provides a full-time college counselor in the school, supports college trips, and helps with every aspect of the college process, including financial aid. In addition, teachers in East Side advisory groups help students think through their pathways after high school, using an inquiry-based multi-year curriculum from the nonprofit College Access: Research and Action (Cara NYC).

As of 2013, New York City determines whether students are "college ready" with an algorithm of standardized assessments that indicates a student will not need remedial courses at the City University of New York (CUNY). By 2014, East Side graduates were almost twice as likely as the average New York City high school graduate to have that college-ready status (56 percent versus 33 percent). That same year, 69 percent of East Side graduates enrolled in a college or other postsecondary program within six months (compared to the city average of 51 percent), and one-fifth of those were to attend a four-year CUNY college.

Sustaining a Strong Faculty

The East Side faculty remains remarkably stable. Although teachers occasionally leave for family reasons or further education, attrition remains minimal. When a position does arise, collaborative teams of East Side teachers take the lead in hiring the replacement.

As in all public schools, recent years have seen an increased emphasis on teacher evaluation, but at East Side that process reflects the developmental values of the school. For the yearly assessments of professional growth that New York City now requires, the school uses not just the district's eight standards (deriving from the Danielson Framework for Teaching) but also the homegrown "East Side 9." These goals focus explicitly on instructional practices that meet the learning needs of all students, inculcate the school's signature habits of mind, and promote equity and social justice in the classroom. Half of a teacher's evaluation emerges from frequent informal classroom visits in which a designated supervisor provides feedback and invites teacher response. "We aim to cultivate our teachers, not to devastate them," said Federman.

The other half of the evaluation, however, derives from the reflective practices of teachers themselves. Twice yearly in a two-day process, they review their progress and set new goals, based on self-assessment and reflection, collegial observation and feedback, student surveys, professional learning groups, visits to other schools, and more. Additional responsibilities, such as advisory leadership or contributions to the community, further add to their professional portfolio.

'The Future of Ourselves'

The academic depth that East Side students display in their graduation portfolio defenses results, in large part, from the social and emotional supports that surround them from the time they enter East Side. As the school shows that it cares about the well-being of their charges, one teacher concluded, it also signals that "we're taking them seriously intellectually—giving them rich and challenging questions to think about, and taking an interest in their ideas."

When young people start to make personal choices based on such inquiry as well, they are building the sense of agency so crucial to an adolescent's development. In Facing History's terms, they begin to act as "upstanders" rather than "bystanders"—shaping their own lives and affecting the lives of others. As one student put it, "Everything that we learn here at East Side eventually comes to help us out in the future of ourselves and in the future generations that look up to us."

EXHIBIT 2.1   ROLES AND RESPONSIBILITIES OF EAST SIDE ADVISERS

COMMUNICATING WITH FAMILY

The adviser is the main person responsible for communicating information to parents/guardians. The adviser is responsible for:

- **Communicating regularly with parent** in regard to each advisee's academic progress, behavior, and attendance.
  - Sharing positive updates with parents about the advisee.
  - Informing parents about missing work.
  - Informing parents about behavior issues and consequences. (It is the adviser's job to notify parents about DT.)
- **Updating all changes in contact information** by e-mailing AP and copying her assistant.
- **Ensuring that each parent has a PupilPath username and password** and knows how to access their children's grades. (In cases where the family has no access to a computer, the adviser is responsible for making sure family receives regular PupilPath updates.)
- **Creating, maintaining, and using an advisory parent e-mail list** or PupilPath for communication.
- **Encouraging families to attend all school activities and events**, especially mandated conferences and roundtables.

MONITORING ACADEMIC PERFORMANCE AND PROGRESS

- **Keeping track of each advisee's academic performance** via PupilPath, kid-talk meetings, and communication with teachers.
- **Meeting regularly with advisees** to discuss this info and review goals.
- **Ensuring that each child has a PupilPath username and password** and a time and space to access it.
- **Creating, implementing, and monitoring a Student Support Plan** for each advisee (including tracking goals, after-school, morning study groups, homework and work completion, extracurricular commitments, etc.).

ENSURING ATTENDANCE

The adviser is the main person responsible for monitoring and proactively addressing their advisees' attendance.

- If a parent/guardian does not communicate with the adviser when the student is absent, the adviser must contact them via phone, e-mail, or text.
  1. The first two times a student is absent in a month the adviser must communicate with the family.

EXHIBIT 2.1   *(continued)*

2. The third time in a month that a student is absent the adviser must fill out an Absence (Repeated) anecdotal on PupilPath and a counselor or AP will call home and document the communication and reasoning in the PupilPath.

3. The fourth time in a month that a student is absent the adviser must fill out an Absence (Repeated) anecdotal on PupilPath and the principal will call home and document the communication and reasoning in PupilPath.

- This cycle repeats each month. However, the second time an attendance issue makes it to the AP, the family must be brought in.

SUPPORTING POSITIVE BEHAVIOR

The adviser is the main person responsible for monitoring and proactively addressing a student's behavior issues. The adviser is the first person to deal with instances or patterns of commendable or inappropriate behavior by the student. The adviser is responsible for proactively addressing these behaviors through providing recognition and incentives, implementing consequences for all level I incidents (and notifying the teacher who wrote the report), developing strategies and plans, and seeking services of others.

CONNECTING WITH ADVISEES

It is the responsibility of the adviser to get to know each advisee as best as possible. This includes knowing them as a student and a person.

- **Creating a system** that allows the adviser to have one-on-one or small-group time with each advisee. (See Best Advisory Practices sheet for more ideas.)
- **Being aware** of advisees' interests, needs, passions, and goals
- **Knowing the "temperature"** of advisees

CONNECT ADVISEES TO RESOURCES

The adviser is an advocate for each advisee and is expected to assist in connecting the child to resources that will support her/his academic performance in school as well as her/his general interests and well-being.

- **Reading morning announcements** with the purpose of connecting your advisees with extracurricular activities.
- **Supporting advisees** to advocate for the academic and social-emotional support that they need in order to be successful.

EXHIBIT 2.1   *(continued)*

- Implementing and monitoring the **College Bound Portfolio** with the purpose of getting your advisees more active and well rounded.
- Ensuring that each advisee has a productive **plan for the summer**.

TEACHING ADVISORY CLASS

The adviser is responsible for teaching a class that addresses the following curriculum strand:

- Work habits
- 100% Respect
- Health and healthy relationships
- College bound
- Connecting with your advisees

Courtesy of East Side Community School

EXHIBIT 2.2   100 PERCENT RESPECT BEHAVIORS AT EAST SIDE

Student-to-Student Behaviors

1. Treat people how you would like to be treated.
2. Don't interrupt your peers.
3. Always try to communicate using appropriate language; no cursing.
4. No gossiping or spreading rumors.
5. No instigating.
6. No bullying—physically, emotionally, or psychologically.
7. No fighting.
8. No sexual harassment: physical or verbal.
9. Respect each other's personal property and space.
10. Don't steal.
11. Respect everyone regardless or color, gender, nationality, sexual orientation, age, or individual characteristics.

Student-to-Teacher Behaviors

1. Follow all school rules and procedures.
2. Come to class prepared with all materials; no excuses.
3. Give full attention to the person speaking.
4. Try to compromise.
5. Take responsibility for your actions.
6. No stereotyping of the adults.
7. No cursing.
8. Speak with a reasonable tone or voice.
9. Use positive language and tone of voice ("Please"; "Thank you"; no rolling eyes).
10. Remember to take care of your personal hygiene.
11. Respect teachers' and school's spaces and property.
12. No sexual harassment: physical or verbal.
13. Respect everyone regardless of color, gender, nationality, sexual orientation, age, or individual characteristics.

Teacher-to-Student Behaviors

1. Make lessons interesting.
2. Include all students in lessons/teach to the whole class.
3. Listen to your students.

EXHIBIT 2.2   *(continued)*

4. Always listen to both sides of the story.

5. Respect students' ideas: let them express their voices.

6. Don't play favorites.

7. Don't put students down.

8. Encourage students: use more commendable behavior reports.

9. Don't shout students out: not about grades, nor personal information.

10. Keep professional and personal boundaries clear.

11. Remember to take care of personal hygiene.

12. Don't be hypocritical: take your own advice.

13. Respect students' personal space and property.

14. No sexual harassment: physical or verbal.

15. Don't stereotype kids by the way they look or dress.

16. Respect everyone regardless of color, gender, nationality, sexual orientation, age, or individual characteristics.

Courtesy of East Side Community School

EXHIBIT 2.3   ROUNDTABLE MATH RUBRIC

Student's Name	Evaluator's Name	Date

This student is attempting to satisfy the *communication requirement* for

☐ Algebra   ☐ Geometry
☐ Advanced Algebra
☐ Data Analysis and Probability

ROUNDTABLE EVALUATION RUBRIC

Please check the appropriate boxes and circle an overall rating for each of the three categories

	EXPERT	PRACTITIONER	APPRENTICE	NOVICE
Math Language *How well does this student use and understand math vocabulary?*	☐ Used appropriate math vocabulary *fluently* throughout the presentation. ☐ Correctly and clearly defined terms in their own words (when needed) to make the presentation clear.	☐ Used math vocabulary correctly throughout the majority of the presentation. ☐ Correctly defined terms in their own words when needed. ☐ May have received *minimal* support to clarify definitions.	☐ Occasionally used math vocabulary correctly. ☐ Was unfamiliar with or misused important math vocabulary.	☐ Was unfamiliar with most of the relevant math vocabulary.

EXHIBIT 2.3   *(continued)*

Problem Solving *How well does this student solve "pure" math problems connected to this big idea?*	□ Correctly solved complex problems *independently*. □ Explained all of the solution steps, precisely, using math language.	□ Clearly demonstrated that they understood how to solve the problem(s) they presented. □ May have received *minimal* support pointing out a calculation error or a simple mistake.	□ *Partially* understood how to solve the problem(s) presented. □ Needed significant support that showed that they were not yet ready to solve these types of problems independently.	□ Needed a level of support that indicated that they do not yet understand how to solve this type of problem.
Applications/ Connections *How well does this student apply the math concept to solve a "real world" problem or complete an interesting project?*	□ *Thoroughly* and clearly explained their process for solving the application problem or completing the project.	□ Clearly demonstrated that they understood how to apply this math concept to solve the problem or complete the project.	□ *Partially* understood how to apply this math concept to solve the problem or complete the project.	□ Needed a level of support that indicated that they do not yet understand how to apply this math concept to solve the problem or complete the project.

	Expert	Practitioner	Apprentice	Novice
OR How well can this student connect this math concept to another math topic?	☐ Clearly explained *why* this math concept could be applied in this context. AND/OR ☐ Provided a sophisticated explanation of how one mathematical idea is connected to another.	☐ May have received *minimal* support pointing out a calculation error or a simple mistake. OR ☐ Clearly explained how this math concept is connected to another.	☐ Needed significant support that showed that they were not yet ready to independently apply the math to this context. OR ☐ *Partially* explained how this math concept is connected to another.	OR ☐ Needed a level of support that indicated that they do not yet understand how to connect this math concept to another.

Overall Evaluation (circle one)   Expert   Practitioner   Apprentice   Novice

What strengths did the student demonstrate? _____

_____

Describe the support the student needed during the presentation (be specific): _____

_____

Courtesy of East Side Community School

CHAPTER 3

"Raising Scholars, Inside Out"

Quest Early College High School
Humble, Texas

IDEA AND CONTEXT

Six teenagers sit in a small conference room at Quest Early College High School in Humble (pronounced "umble"), Texas, clearly comfortable with each other and the questions of visitors. They take turns telling what makes this small, innovative district school so different from the large comprehensive high schools that serve the rest of Humble's roughly nine thousand high school students.

"We're like a family here," says Keith, a lanky, voluble sophomore. "Or maybe a clan with lots of families."

"What makes this school stand out for me is service," says Andrew, another tenth grader, who spends a day each week as a teacher's aide at a nearby elementary school. He shares his proudest moment: teaching eight-year-old Austin how to read. "When I was young, I wasn't great at reading," he says. "He reminded me of myself."

"What comes to mind for me is the tight relationship you have with the facilitators [teachers]," says Kidist, an eleventh grader who moved from Ethiopia to Houston at age thirteen and "ran right out the door" when she toured the district's large high schools.

"I like the freedom and the responsibility," says Tanya, who has been quiet until now. "They give you lots of choices, the students plan all of the clubs, we decide what we'll do in family, no one tells you what to do. But it means you're 100 percent responsible, too. You feel mature."

Jordan remembers losing friends in middle school because he took algebra at the high school. "The other kids would say, 'Don't be with that guy, he's weird,'" he says. "They made me feel ashamed. Then I came here and kids would say, 'Wow, that freshman is in Algebra 2. He's kinda cool.' I felt like I belonged."

Small by Design

One hundred years ago—before the discovery of oil in Humble temporarily turned the town into the largest oilfield in Texas—the Humble Independent School District consisted of a one-room schoolhouse with twelve students, a teacher, and a four-month school term. It's been growing ever since, with good schools a prime asset in this suburban community twenty-five miles north of downtown Houston.

At last count, Humble ISD was the largest "industry" in the area, with forty-one schools, and over forty thousand students and five thousand employees. In 2011 and 2012, Harris County, into which the district juts, added more residents than any other county in the United States. For more than a decade, Humble ISD has been one of the fastest-growing school districts in Texas. Three of its five comprehensive high schools, with enrollments ranging from one thousand five hundred to three thousand one hundred students, were built between 2006 and 2009. Before that, Humble High School (founded in 1918) had swelled to over five thousand students.

The population influx and the large high schools it has produced are deep points of local pride. This is Texas, where, as one Quest student put it, "Bigger is better." Schools are ranked by their size—from one A (1A) to five A's (5A)—and whether competing for football or mathematics, schools match up with others their size and the 5A trophies carry the most weight.

So when Quest opened with fewer than two hundred students in 1995, its founders—a group of local educators inspired by the growing national small schools movement—were making a bold wager: that bigger was not always better. The experimental school offered a stark contrast to nearby Kingwood High School, where the gleaming strut of the Military Marching Band, alone, engaged almost twice as many students.

Then as now, the schools here in suburban Houston seemed to work just fine. The district dropout rate was less than 3.5 percent, attendance hovered around 96 percent, 90 percent of students passed the state proficiency exams, college admission rates at the two comprehensive high schools were excellent, and the football teams regularly won the state championships.

Yes, the high schools were enormous, district leaders said, but virtually any student could find a niche in the extensive extracurricular organizations they provided.

Yet not all students thrived in such conventional large high schools, the district leadership acknowledged. Many students slipped through the cracks: students whose strengths matched poorly with eight-period days, traditional pedagogy, and "shopping-mall" course selections in which teachers could rarely get to know students well. For some students, to adjust socially seemed to require a more personal setting—one that Texas educator and visionary Thomas Sergiovanni called "communitarian."[1] Humble's assistant superintendent at the time agreed. "For some students," he said, "the large traditional high school spells disaster."

Quest promised an alternative. After a year of reading, thinking, and visiting innovative schools nationwide, the school's planning team (with the support of the assistant superintendent) settled on a set of design principles aligned with Theodore R. Sizer's cutting-edge Coalition of Essential Schools. They included teaching loads (fewer than eighty students) that made it possible to know every student well. A vision of students as workers and teachers as coaches. Personalized teaching and curriculum. Advisories. Graduation by exhibition. An atmosphere of trust and respect. A full embrace of democratic practices and diversity.

To turn these principles into action, the group recruited Kimberly Huseman, a highly regarded teacher who had recently begun connecting students with local service opportunities to increase their engagement and motivation. Huseman promptly convinced the school's planners to include an additional element in the new school's design: setting aside a full day in the Quest weekly schedule for students to serve as volunteers in the community.

The business of where the school would reside had already been settled. A year earlier, the district had issued a bond to house under one roof several alternative programs for at-risk youth, including kids in trouble with the law, pregnant students, and English language learners. While the students entering Quest would not be at risk by these measures, the new Community Learning Center, the district reasoned, would be a suitable home for students unhappy in a large high school. (Ironically, a few years later Quest moved to a wing of one of the district's biggest high schools.)

As the school welcomed its first students, excitement—and skepticism—ran high.

"The school's founders were convinced the school would take hold—indeed that it would become a national laboratory for best practices," said current Quest principal Ginger Noyes, who was part of the original faculty and then served as assistant principal until 2012. "The skeptics, of which there were many, were convinced we'd lost our minds."

Serving the Whole Child

At Quest, knowing every child well meant educating the whole child. "For us, they've always been one and the same," said Noyes. When Quest won the Association for Supervision and Curriculum Development's Vision in Action Whole Child Award in 2011, the school felt both honored and vindicated in its long drive to create a school where the social and emotional needs of students mattered as much as their intellect. The school had come to shine academically. In 2011, Quest led the district's five other high schools when it came to daily attendance (96 percent), the pass rate on state proficiency exams (almost 100 percent), and student retention (94 percent)—winning begrudging praise from those who continued to view the school as an outlier.

The ASCD award pointed to an additional set of strengths. It recognized Quest for the school's move beyond a narrow focus on academic achievement to "take action for the whole child, creating learners who are knowledgeable, emotionally and physically healthy, civically active, artistically engaged, prepared for economic self-sufficiency, and ready for the real world beyond formal schooling." The commendation also noted that Quest's commitment to the social and emotional growth of students was rare at the high school level.

Unsaid, but also noteworthy, Quest had built and made these strides with an increasingly diverse student body—against an educational landscape where race, ethnicity, and class chronically separate students. At Kingwood High School five miles to the north, 77 percent of the 2,659 students were white and only 6 percent met federal poverty guidelines in 2011. Eight miles to the south at Summer Creek High School, just 17 percent of the 1,980 students were white, and over half were eligible for free or reduced lunch. At Quest in 2011, 43 percent of the 221 students were white, and the remainder were Hispanic, African American, and Asian; 43 percent met federal poverty guidelines.

When Quest twelfth graders picked a social justice topic for their senior project, the by-products of inequality invariably drew their attention. "I don't know if that falls into the category of getting us ready for the real world," quipped Bekele, "but reading [Barbara Ehrenreich's] *Nickel and Dimed* sure opened my eyes to poverty in a new way."

Early College

At the time of the school's ASCD Whole Child award, Quest framed its six core beliefs about teaching and learning in these words:

- We should educate the whole child by valuing social, emotional, physical, and academic learning.
- A learning community shall be respectful and safe where all are nurtured and valued.
- Integrity, responsibility, persistence, creativity, and hard work are keys to success in high school, college, and life.
- Teaching, learning, scholarship, and service extend beyond the classroom.
- Students become responsible for their own success when they are taught the process of thinking and learning.
- People have the power to make a difference in their local, national, and global communities and to be advocates for themselves and others.

But a seventh belief was already in the works:

- Our students can successfully complete a high school and college curriculum and be lifelong learners when utilizing deliberate and consistent structures and systems.

Just as the decision to devote one day a week to service learning had been pivotal to Quest's trajectory when it started, the school's 2010 decision to become an early college high school marked a turn in the road for Quest.

Despite the school's successes, the Humble school board remained skeptical of Quest, uneasy about its small size (at the time it cost more per pupil although now it costs less) and its nontraditional curriculum.

The Early College High School (ECHS) model, on the other hand, had the board's favor, and becoming an early college high school promised a lifeline for Quest and new opportunities for students. Already there were 15 early college high schools in Greater Houston and more than 240 nationwide.

Launched in 2002 by the Bill & Melinda Gates Foundation among others, early college high schools were designed so that low-income youth, first-generation college goers, English language learners, students of color, and other young people underrepresented in higher education could simultaneously earn a high school diploma and an associate's degree or up to two years of credit toward a bachelor's degree—tuition free.

So when Quest opened for the 2010–2011 school year, it had a new name, Quest Early College High School, and a new home, on the expanding campus of Lone Star Community College. The previous spring, Quest staff and students had made a special effort to recruit incoming ninth graders who would be the first in their families to go to college.

"I hope you didn't mind being the guinea pigs," Noyes said in 2013 to a group of seniors who had been freshmen when early college started. "You took the brunt of all of our learning lessons." But these students figured early on that they were guinea pigs, they told their principal. It was a bonding by ordeal, which brought them closer. Besides, they said, it might turn out fine.

Here, we examine the results of Quest's fierce determination, spanning twenty years, to know each student well, support what makes them whole, challenge students intellectually, and fuel their independence—in a culture where most believe big is better and one size should fit all.

THE SCHOOL IN ACTION

Anyone who doubted the inextricable nature of social, emotional, and academic learning would find abundant evidence of it after spending time at Quest. In every moment of their days, students are immersed in developmental experiences that have them actively building knowledge and making meaning through reflection. Although the contexts vary—as we will see in the examples that follow—the school purposefully engages adolescents in a continuing cycle that leads them, step by step, from first encountering a situation to finally integrating new understanding into their own actions.

A Sense of Belonging

When Ryan, a quiet eighth grader, made an exploratory visit to QECHS, his parents did all of the talking. Gwen Geiser, the Quest recruitment coordinator, had encountered this scene before. On one side sat parents, sold on Quest—perhaps because of its academic push, its small size, its reputation for developing maturity and responsibility in teens, or their worry that their youngster was losing the way. On the other side sat an early adolescent, far from convinced: *What would my friends think? Isn't this a school for nerds or misfits? Do I really want to study that hard? How can a high school have no team sports? Would I fit in? Do I want to fit in?*

Ryan and his parents would have to sign the QECHS contract, requiring students to complete their challenging academic work and study two to three hours a night. As Geiser went through its terms, she saw Ryan stiffen. "What if I don't like it?" he asked. She had given the answer to applicants countless times: "Stay a year, to give it a heartfelt try." This time, as often happened, it meant the student would not agree to come.

Quest uses a rubric to help sort through applications (see Exhibit 3.1). At the top of its list are students who would be the first in their family to attend college or are economically disadvantaged, but willingness to work hard follows closely. Applicants are encouraged to visit Quest, not to tour its facilities but to "feel the hum."

Whether they come to Quest with ambivalence or eagerness, most new students are ready to seek affirmation and belonging in a high school far smaller than others in this district. Jordan, whom we met earlier, felt worn down by peers taunting him about his math precocity. Katie said she had all the "supposed tos" together: cheerleader, junior varsity team leader, student council member, straight A's. But she wanted to make her own path.

Since its earliest days, Quest has prioritized a strong school community where all students feel that they belong. That sense of having a place in one's group constitutes a basic human need, as psychologist Abraham Maslow noted long ago. Because human learning is socially constructed through interactions with others, feeling part of a community of learners has a strongly motivating effect in schools. Considerable research supports the connection between students' sense of belonging in a classroom or school and their academic performance.[2]

The school's size (around 225 students for many years and 350 in 2014–2015) would seem to ensure feelings of belonging. Yet its students come from eight district middle schools that are not as diverse as they will find at Quest. Before the fall semester starts, a weeklong Bridge Camp inducts new students into the school's distinctive community. Students spend five days rotating between Socratic seminars, games, trust exercises, cardio workouts, relationship building, talks on growth mind-set, relaxation techniques, and just plain fun. They also receive intensive tutoring before taking, on the last day of camp, the Texas Success Initiative test, which qualifies them to take college courses.

"I came in pretty much not knowing anybody and wondering if I'd made a mistake," said one ninth grader, whose parents were split on whether she should attend Quest, with the girl falling somewhere in between. She left with three new friends and "ready to go," she said. (Quest also runs a short Bridge Camp for parents to help them understand the school's emphasis on the whole child, perseverance, and mastery rather than grades.)

Building Social and Emotional Ties

The heart and soul of Quest, students and teachers often declared in our conversations, are the mixed-age advisory groups known as "family," which meet daily for half an hour. On the first day of school, students are randomly assigned to families, each with a facilitator (the term for teachers at Quest) and approximately fifteen students in grades nine through twelve.

No one picks her or his family members, principal Noyes reminds students. Welcoming difference is an explicit norm at Quest, which has zero tolerance for exclusive groups and cliques. "Put-downs and push-outs aren't acceptable here," said Alycia, an eleventh grader. "I've learned how to relate to people I never really would've been friends with before. And when they graduate and leave, you feel like you've lost a sibling."

Each family—twenty in all in the fall of 2014—charts its own course within a common set of expectations that students will participate, act with respect, venture outside their comfort zone, and support one another. Students help plan each day's activities. Sometimes they begin with a game that gets everyone on their feet. On one warm October day, a group knelt in a circle, crossed hands, and then tried to keep them clasped as they rose to their tiptoes. In the classroom next door, "sighted" students worked with blindfolded partners to put together large jigsaw puzzles.

Sometimes, family starts with a discussion. Students in social studies facilitator Jim Nerad's family talked about what they had given up by not attending a large high school filled with extracurricular activities. "I wish the school had an orchestra," a ninth-grade girl said. "I play the violin, and the orchestra in my middle school, like, kept me motivated. Now it seems like I have no time, you know, no urge to pick up my violin. It makes me sad." A boy next to her wished he could learn about game design, but he couldn't find enough other students who shared his interest. Another student spoke wistfully of the varsity swimming that had filled her afternoons, which she was trying to make up in a weekend swim club.

A staple in many families is a ritual they call "connections." Students sit in a circle and anyone with something to say may speak uninterrupted. Sometimes students share a personal accomplishment. Other times they ask for advice. Predictably, the invitation to open up in a safe space, with peers who wish you well, deepens the talking and listening. One student described a bad fight he'd had with his parents the night before. Another spoke of her ongoing feelings that she's "not smart enough." A third related a misunderstanding with her boss, which made her not want to go back to work.

Sometimes these conversations yield advice or possible solutions. Just as important, the connections normalize the struggles that students go through. Young people see that their peers also have difficulties; they learn that setbacks are part of growing up. Not surprisingly, research suggests that loneliness and alienation, to the extent to which they are associated with academic work, drain a student's engagement in learning.[3] "Here you have a classroom full of kids you can talk to and say how you feel," Tanya explained.

In some families, mentoring relationships between students in upper and lower grades also become part of the structure. Pairs find their own rhythms—there is no protocol—in a two-way exchange. "Even though they're younger than you," said Katie, a twelfth grader, "they have a different mind-set and a different opinion. And you learn from them, too."

Making Service Learning Core

It was Friday morning and instead of lugging backpacks to class Quest students were traveling light, jumping into buses that would take them to the service sites where they would spend the next four hours. They fanned out across the area—to elementary schools, a center for disabled young adults, an animal shelter, a hospital clinic, a nursing home, and more.

At Jesse Jones Park, an oasis of small forests and fields a twenty-five-minute drive from the school, one group known as the Green Team served as environmental stewards. Eleven miles away at Elm Grove Elementary School, Katie was tutoring a third grader, who had just told her there was no point to school. "I'm just gonna go to work," he said. Katie seized the occasion to start a conversation with the child about grit.

James, who has a brother with autism, worked elbow to elbow with two disabled young adults at the Cambridge Center. As they rolled out the dough for dog biscuits, he drew them into conversation about pet peeves. At the nearby Texas Medical Center, half a dozen students greeted patients as they entered the large waiting room. The students offered water or coffee, eased the restlessness of young children waiting with an ill parent, and answered patients' questions about what to expect.

When asked what they value most about their school, Quest students put service right after family, if not ahead. Passionate about community service, the school's founding principal allocated one day a week to service learning long before such hours showed up on other high school transcripts. Twenty years later, the tradition remains vital to Quest's mission.

Students volunteer at an array of sites where Quest has built steady relationships. Like Katie, many find their place at one of the district's elementary schools. They move quickly from helping a teacher with chores to working directly with groups of kids or individual students—teaching them to read, to speak English, to multiply, to persevere. Twelfth graders may pursue an internship on their own, with the school's backing. Or they can elect to become a service-learning leader assigned to a particular site; they alternate between observing classmates at work and providing feedback one week, then joining the action the next week. They receive special training for their observation duties, using a rubric developed for this purpose.

As well as reflecting aloud on their service in the family group, students complete written reflections on it at the end of each semester. They also evaluate themselves in four categories: attendance (e.g., consistent), attitude (e.g., exercised good judgment), learning process (e.g., showed initiative), performance (e.g., handled constructive criticism well). (See Exhibit 3.2.) Their adult supervisor evaluates the students using the same standards; service is a credit-bearing course.

Though many schools strive to link service learning to the academic curriculum, here the ties to social and emotional learning matter most. Asked to make a list of what they had gained, a group of seniors talked about learning to relate to people of different ages and backgrounds, to communicate better one-on-one and publicly, to take initiative and assume responsibility, to show patience, to reach out without being asked, to think ahead. It seems intuitive that for adolescents—at an age when idealism and justice compete with self-absorption—the belief that their contributions matter would go a long way to making them feel valued. Youth grow in important ways when adults in the community invite and salute their contributions, research suggests.[4] The forty developmental assets identified by the Search Institute as critical to youth ages twelve to eighteen include promoting equality and reducing hunger and poverty, helping others, acting on convictions, and having a sense of purpose.[5]

"When I came to Quest, I saw Fridays as a day I didn't have to go to class and could, you know, knock off," James admitted. "Now I don't just want to make an impact in my community, but all around the world if I can."

Teachers as Facilitators

As an early member of Theodore R. Sizer's Coalition of Essential Schools (CES), Quest embraced that movement's ten common principles, which used the metaphors of "student as worker" and "teacher as coach." Rather than simply delivering instructional services, CES advised, teachers should "provoke students to learn how to learn and thus to teach themselves." At Quest, teachers have consistently nurtured not only their students' academic growth but also their development as healthy adolescents and conscientious citizens. From the school's start, Quest teachers have always been called facilitators.

Coach, parent, friend, tutor, cheerleader, nudge, standard-bearer, connector, advocate, and, of course, teacher—facilitators at Quest play all of these roles. A typical day includes tutoring students when they arrive at 8:00 but before classes start at 8:45; teaching several subject-area classes; overseeing family; leading a daily section of AVID (Advancement via Individual Determination, a highly regarded study skills and college readiness course required of all Quest students); supervising a student-led club; speaking individually with students and often their parents. On Fridays, when students head to their service-learning placements, faculty meet for three hours as a professional learning community and then catch up with paperwork and planning.

New staff members can find the school's family structure off-putting; little in their training has taught them how to facilitate the fluidity of this student-led space. They sometimes question how game playing and open discussion relate to learning algebra or writing a research paper. By all accounts, however, they quickly adapt as they observe veteran Quest staff and discuss strategies during weekly meetings of their professional learning community. "They realize that the relationships they build with students in family is what helps students take risks, persevere, and soar," said Ginger Noyes. "They learn firsthand what the research tells us: students recognize and try hard for a teacher that cares."[6]

Learning how to be participants rather than potentates in the classroom presents an even bigger challenge to teachers. New to Quest, Danielle Maldonado described her natural preference for lecturing. "That was what I was used to as a student, and—I thought—how I learned best," she said. "I resisted group work; I resisted all these techniques that I thought were just wasting time. But there was no way lecturing would work as a teaching strategy at this school."

She thought hard about how she could go beyond simply feeding her students information. "I decided that the best way students learn is by teaching," she said. Now, "Half of the time they are in front of the classroom and I'm seated in back."

When it came to teaching chemistry, Valerie Booth, another new teacher, turned to a framework called POGIL (for Process Oriented Guided Inquiry Learning) developed by the National Science Foundation. Using carefully designed materials and guided inquiry—a learning cycle of exploration, concept invention, and application—she has students construct their own understanding, or as Booth put it, "their own 'aha' moments." Students work in small groups with assigned roles that promote full engagement in the learning process. At the end of each class, a reporter describes the process skills that helped her or his group work as a team that day, along with the concepts they grasped and the ones they didn't. Booth then uses the feedback to plan the next POGIL.

"Plus I mix it up," Booth added. She asks students what their class notes would look like if she *had* lectured and then has them create those notes for homework and compare them with teammates the next day. "Their understanding of core concepts in chemistry—the 'aha' moments—keeps growing," she said.

Jamie Knox had taught theater in college before joining Quest, where she is the school's only elective teacher and theater the only elective. Faced with a class of high school students for whom theater was a hard sell, she used participatory activities such as Socratic seminars—with their open-ended discussions about a text—and "philosophical chairs"—an AVID strategy in which students debate a topic that is important to them—in teaching students to analyze a script, pick out what's important, compare plays, and more. For a midterm review, she created a "gallery walk" with three whiteboards: one for Greek tragedy, another for Shakespeare, a third for basic staging. Students who felt they were experts on one of the topics were invited to go to that board and write down as much as they knew. Then the whole class moved from board to board, taking notes and posting questions, which the student experts answered in turn.

"I want my students to know that their voices and their ideas are important, that there's someone listening to them, that they can be experts if they try," said Knox.

The Importance of Mastery Learning

In a 2012 paper on the role of noncognitive factors in adolescent learning, researchers at the Chicago Consortium on School Research identified the critical factors that underpin student success in middle and high school. They grouped those factors into five general categories: academic behaviors, academic perseverance, academic mind-sets, social skills, and learning strategies.

"School performance is a complex phenomenon, shaped by a wide variety of factors intrinsic to students and in their external environment," the authors noted. In addition to content knowledge and academic skills, "students must develop sets of behaviors, skills, attitudes, and strategies that are crucial to academic performance in their classes."[7]

At Quest, these skills, behaviors, mind-sets, and strategies are bundled into the term *mastery learning*, a hallmark of its approach since the school's start.

Delicate in appearance, facilitator Mishka Douglas—a Quest graduate herself—is known for being quirky and tough. She has a habit of asking her ninth-grade English students an open-ended question; as students offer answers, she tells each one, "You're right." They find her response annoying, but they get her point: many questions have no single answer.

"I have higher expectations than a lot of the students are used to," said Douglas. "They come here from middle school with straight A's, versed in regurgitating the 'right' answer. Maybe they've been taught that, say, they're a good writer, and then their first assignment with me they don't pass. All of a sudden it's 'What? Either I've become stupid or the teacher is bad.'" Douglas wants her students to work hard for their grades. "Few of us are born knowing how to write a good introductory paragraph," she tells them. "But if you do it over and over again, you'll figure it out."

Most ninth graders who enroll at Quest arrive tuned, at least, to receive Douglas's message. At Bridge Camp, they hear it loud and clear: it's not about talent but about how hard you are willing to work to get what you want. When asked what they thought set them apart from classmates in middle school, many Quest students talked about drive.

"In my middle school, other kids looked at kids like us as nerds or overachievers," said Keith. "Working hard wasn't cool. Here you're with other people who have the drive; it helps keep you going. At Quest we all wanna go different places and accomplish different things, but the thing is that we wanna go!"

Even with drive, challenges as well as opportunities come with a growth mind-set. It may be reassuring that one can master trigonometry with effort, even without the math gene. But the decision remains how much effort to make. Although Quest students sign a contract pledging to work hard, they may underestimate the bargain.

In "normal" high school (the adjective both students and staff use to describe the other high schools in Humble ISD), kids often blow off hard work and get away with it, three tenth graders agreed. At Quest, "it catches up with you fast," said Jordan. "There's no such thing as 'I'm not good at that' and checking out."

"Sometimes I've worked so hard that my head hurts," added Melissa, "and my teacher will say, 'Good, that means you're learning.'"

Facilitators do everything they can to help students persist, including allaying the fears of parents who burden their children with their own anxieties about less-than-perfect grades—anxieties that are endemic in a community like Humble where grade-point averages are akin to a competitive sport.

Each morning before school begins, a rotating group of facilitators is available to tutor students. During a twenty-minute "tenth period," also at the start of school, facilitators meet one-on-one with individual students. In class, facilitators become practiced at scaffolding the learning process. They always build choice into their courses, encouraging students to select assignments that are just right—not so challenging that they risk discouragement, not so easy that they court boredom. When students do poorly on a test, they may always retake it for a better score, and a homework assignment isn't incomplete until a unit ends.

Progress is relative. "One student's growth may be exponential," said Knox, "but it may only be the beginning. They all start in such different places, you can't compare them. You have to keep going back and remember where they came from." Yet mastery is always the goal, however long it takes.

"I guess you'd call it a mantra here: helping students grow their competence through effort," said assistant principal Janette Horton. Yet that cannot happen without emotional support, as Mishka Douglas remarked: "Unless students know you care, unless you tell them you are supporting them, it may be hard for them to keep going or to find their own motivation."

Independent Learning and AVID

In the fall of 2013, Quest joined the other high schools in the district as a site for AVID, a system that uses Socratic seminars and a variety of other methods to teach skills related to organization, note taking, speaking, writing, and inquiry. AVID's success in nurturing self-regulated learners and metacognitive skills seemed a good fit at Quest, especially given the college coursework students here must complete to receive their high school diploma. While the other five district high schools made AVID an elective, Quest required it of every ninth and tenth grader the first year and of students in all grades starting in the fall of 2014. In 2013 the course met twice a week for ninety minutes. Now it meets four days a week, including two ninety-minute blocks—an affirmation of the central place AVID has come to occupy in the curriculum. All of the school's faculty and administration have received intensive AVID training at the state level.

Initially, many staff and students at Quest found AVID prescriptive and tedious. A year later, they had come to see the program as a toolbox with easily adaptable "success strategies."

One AVID protocol requires students to submit, in advance of class, a form in which they describe a "point of confusion" in one of their other courses. The AVID facilitator uses that information to divide students into inquiry groups of four or five. Within each group, students take turns outlining their confusion on a flip chart and inviting peers to help sort it out with questions or strategies; college students serve as tutors for the groups.

In Kathy Moss's AVID class, for example, groups of students had written these points of confusion on their flip charts:

- If you have wavelength in cm, identify what you multiply to do dimensional analyses.
- How do you use the "me" conjugation with reflexive verbs? [Spanish]
- Compare and contrast the Persian Empire to the Roman Empire.
- How many valence electrons would transition metals have?
- How do I create a mnemonic device to remember suffixes?

Their peers posed related questions, offering and debating the strategies others offered. Each presenting student in turn jotted down notes on the left side of the flip chart and problem-solving suggestions on the right, while also engaging in the discussion.

Learning to take Cornell notes is another staple of AVID, as are strategies for time management and organization. Students learn how to prioritize assignments, ask for help, work as a team, and work independently. Strategies are scaffolded across the four years (with a focus on skills needed for college and college applications in junior and senior year).

"Students here, many of us go into AVID thinking that we already have a system for doing school that works, we have our planners, we have our A's," said one tenth grader. "But AVID teaches us some new strategies, most of which are better. With the full-strength curriculum you have here, you need full-strength tools."

Everyone's Participation Counts

"So here's the drill," Holly Shoettlin yelled as twenty or so Quest sophomores lined up for "boot camp" on the Lone Star Community College athletic field behind the school. She got them started forming teams of four, picking a mascot, and creating a team cheer. Then she set the task: "Flip these tires to the cones you see down the field and back, with each team member taking a turn."

Shoettlin, herself a kinesthesiologist, leads this thrice-weekly cardiovascular workout that is part of the school's longstanding commitment to wellness. It's not a competition, she told her group that day. "Your job is to support your team members and to make a strong effort. What matters, as always, is your participation."

Whether in boot camp or humanities class, hanging back at Quest is rarely an option. Student participation is considered essential to building both community and social-emotional skills. Even on the organizational chart that the principal must submit to the school district, Noyes made sure that students appeared alongside faculty and administration. "They are integral to our structure," she said. "They give as much as they receive."

Twice weekly, the first block of the day is reserved for student-run clubs. On one October morning, twenty students joined Kidist, an eleventh grader from Ethiopia, in the club she formed to explore women's rights in the developing world. Across the hall, students performed skits in a theater club with no adult direction. Another room filled with students eager to reach out to disabled adults in the community. In an empty parking lot in front of the Lone Star campus, students in a makeshift sports club played pickup soccer, basketball, and dodgeball, with no prior athletic skills required.

The school's Student Ambassador program attracts close to a quarter of the student body. Its participants help facilitate meetings that involve parents or local citizens, visit middle schools to recruit new students, host visitors to the school, and speak publicly on behalf of Quest. They also provide day care for parents who bring young children to their conferences with QECHS staff.

The games students routinely play in family are also part of the culture of participation. Whether or not they like the game, students are expected to participate, even if they only make a gesture. It is purposeful play, intended to build community and trust and to release tension. "Yeah, and it teaches us to have fun," said Jordan. "We can be a pretty serious lot." At lunchtime, students are as often out on the field kicking a ball or playing tag as they are inside eating or huddled in conversation. Ginger Noyes may be the only principal you'll hear telling sixteen- and seventeen-year-olds to go out and play, several Quest staff mused.

As noted earlier, classroom structures at QECHS also pivot on student participation and discussion. The give-and-take in family, with its emphasis on respectful conversation, primes students for the same process to take place in their classes. "The comfort level students feel with each other here is remarkable," said facilitator Jim Nerad. "And it shows up in class discussions, where just about everyone comments and the conversation can run deep."

A Meaningful Curriculum

The college classes that QECHS students take on the Lone Star campus have patent value: credits earned there put them ahead academically and can add up to a tuition-free associate's degree from the college. The instruction from college faculty (mostly lectures) does not always engage them, students said, but they take pride in the fact that they frequently outperform their college classmates on classroom presentations and tests.

They value their high school classes for other reasons, according to Quest facilitators. As considerable research has established, the academic tasks and topics that matter most to students are those that connect somehow to their interests, their future, and their lives. When students value what they are being asked to learn, they are more likely to expend effort mastering it and to persist when the going gets tough. When a task is not valued, students may struggle to focus their attention on it, forget information related to it, or simply give up.[8]

The contract students and parents sign when they enter Quest includes an unlikely clause that bears the heading "Uncensored Curriculum." Students will be expected to participate in "open exchanges of ideas, discussions, debates, and class assignments concerning every possible subject matter," it cautions. "Every QECHS student will assuredly have his or her values and beliefs challenged at various times while enrolled in this program."

As the first book her tenth-grade English class would read in the fall term, facilitator Danielle Maldonado chose George Orwell's *1984*. To prime students for "Big Brother," Maldonado uploaded to the class Web site two provocative newspaper articles about schools using computer chips to track pupils. After reading the articles for homework, students debated the question "Do public school students deserve privacy when it comes to attendance, search, and seizure?"

Three weeks later, the class had analyzed Shelby Steele's essay "The New Sovereignty," about grievance groups becoming nations unto themselves, and had also completed a timed writing about Shirley Jackson's "The Lottery," a chilling tale of conformity gone mad. Having shared their writing and reflections online, students took turns leading classmates through a discussion of a chapter from *1984*. Maldonado encouraged them not to focus overly on the plot but rather to pick a theme they thought stood out. "The idea is pulling out motifs and connecting them to current society, reflecting on what it means today," she said. As part of the school's efforts to help students develop agency and voice, the students also learn and practice the key elements in making a persuasive speech, with help from a rubric (see Exhibit 3.3).

Tucked between two college classrooms on the second floor of the building Quest occupies at the Atascocita Center, a stand-alone campus in the Lone Star Community College system, lies the "flipped" classroom created by Kelly Carruthers, who teaches dual-credit biology, anatomy, and physiology for Quest juniors and seniors. (Courses at QECHS fall into three categories: high school courses like Danielle Maldonado's tenth-grade English; dual-credit courses taught by QECHS faculty certified to teach at the college level; and standard college classes taught by Lone Star faculty.) Carruthers records two twenty-five-minute lectures a week for each class and then students watch the lectures at home, on their own schedule. Class time is reserved for a warm-up exercise (typically an invitation for students to find real-world examples of what they are studying) followed by an activity (often a lab, sometimes a worksheet). "You're always figuring things out in her class," said one biology student, "bouncing ideas off the other kids in your group or Ms. Carruthers. You can hear all the thinking going on."

Meanwhile, students in Jim Nerad's dual-credit Senior Social Action class were discussing Patricia McCormick's *Sold*, the story of Lakshmi, a thirteen-year-old Nepalese girl forced into sexual slavery in India to support her family. The book had so upset one student that she sought out a documentary on human trafficking to understand it better. Another student, who grew up in India, had read the book in one day and felt angry that its theme did not surprise her: "It's a disgrace you get used to, if you live in India."

His students were hungry, said Nerad—always asking for more. They spend first semester immersed in analyses of injustice and inequality nationally and globally; for second semester, they pick a local social action project. "Just go out and find something that has real meaning for you," the teacher told the class. "Go out and meet, talk, interview. Go out and give, go out and learn." The same approach infuses Nerad's Historical Analysis class, where the topics range from First Amendment rights to minimum wage, and the assignments include making "personal masks" (of who you are and hope to become) and demonstrating a social issue through original art. Such work had ample value to his students, by all accounts. "You have this teacher who's been teaching forever," said Bekele. "He knows his stuff, but what he really teaches you is about life."

Becoming Mature

The Collaborative for Academic, Social, and Emotional Learning (CASEL) at the University of Illinois–Chicago identifies five interrelated sets of cognitive, affective, and behavioral competencies that evidence suggests contribute to student growth and mastery. Daniel Goleman's landmark book *Emotional Intelligence* provides the theoretical foundation. The competencies include self-awareness, self-management, social awareness, relationship skills, and responsible decision making.[9]

Faculty members at Quest pointed to those competencies in describing what they hope to achieve with students. Jim Nerad spoke of the social awareness he seeks to stimulate in his action research class with twelfth graders. Assessment coordinator Dolly Covington described coaching self-management skills with students who are falling behind. Ginger Noyes talked about fostering self-regulation and responsible decision making in the student body.

"We have a famous saying here, 'We don't do that at Quest,'" explained Noyes. "And then we say, 'This is why we don't do it.' In six months, you'll see the same kids who were behaving in ways that challenged others now saying, 'We don't do that here.' They become self-regulating."

Quest students, however, boiled down such social and emotional attributes to one ingredient: "becoming mature." Gathered again in the small conference room in the QECHS office, they reflected on what maturity meant to them.

They talked about being treated like adults:

You come from middle school, being treated like you're still in kindergarten, and then all of a sudden you're given these new standards, you know, higher expectations, more responsibility. It's not just free and easy. Far from it. You have to act like an adult to be treated like an adult, and that's what we learn here. —Alycia

They talked about gathering direction in their lives:

When I was in middle school, I started getting irritated with people 'cause I felt they weren't contemplating the consequences of their actions. So I tried coming to Quest and I found a lot of people like myself. Not that they think they're better than other people or that other people are stupid, but they were more on a mature level and they were more thinking about where they wanted to go in life, what they wanted to do with themselves, how they could get there. —Tanya

They talked about growing confidence, most of all in relation to speaking up and becoming a leader:

That's definitely how Quest is. I feel like in eighth grade sitting in this meeting right here, I'd be like, "Oh my goodness! I don't know what to say. I'm so nervous." But I've had so many opportunities to speak about what I'm doing and the program I'm in that I really feel like I've blossomed as a leader, as a speaker, as everything. Because like I said, my knees would be shaking sitting here. —Melissa

They talked about suspending judgment and gaining empathy:

You learn a lot about other people in the world and reflecting on others. In family, my freshman year, it really hit me when fellow freshmen shared their stories about what they were going through, like homelessness or violence. And then service, getting out into the community and meeting kids and other people you'd ordinarily never meet—it really helps you to think about other people and not just what's going on with you in your life. It's, you know, the world. —Andrew

They talked about shedding identities that limited them and using freedom responsibly:

One of the things you learn here is that the identities you have in high school—the athlete, the nerd—disappear when you go on in college and beyond. Part of learning and becoming an adult is shedding these identities and the ways they limit growth and who you can be. —James

Your freshman and sophomore year you get practice, you know, in managing yourself. Then your junior year, you're sent out into a college where freedom is yours to use or abuse. You go because it's your responsibility. You've learned to work hard, to go after what you want, without anyone telling you. —Kidist

They talked about learning to be close to others:

One of the big things you learn in family is how to open up, how to build relationships, how to be close to someone, how to accept who they are and what they do and how to have them accept what you do. It feels great. —Keith

Keith and Alycia and their classmates could recall their qualms when they first started at Quest. They dealt with those worries, they said, because they figured they could always return to "regular" school. A year later, however, they couldn't imagine ever going back.

RESULTS AND SUSTAINABILITY

In 2014, Quest set academic records that topped the charts—as good as the perfect season that nearby high school football teams would vie for. On statewide tests, it ranked better than 98.5 percent of high schools in Texas and first among the six high schools in the Humble Independent School District. (In 2010, Quest's percentile had been 49 percent.) In a community where schools, by and large, were separated by race and class, the student body at Quest remained strikingly diverse. In 2014, 37 percent of Quest students were Hispanic, 35 percent were white, 19 percent were African American, and 36 percent qualified for free or reduced lunch.

On the State of Texas Assessments of Academic Readiness (STAAR) end-of-course exam for Algebra 1, 100 percent of QECHS students were scored as proficient (compared to 86 percent districtwide). Texas has a formula for scoring schools' performance on closing the achievement gap and postsecondary readiness; here Quest ranked in the top 25 percent state-wide, even though 60 percent of its students would be the first in their family to attend college.

The dual-enrollment figures made Quest a standout among early college high schools across the state and within Humble ISD. Seventy percent of its seniors in 2014 graduated with an associate's degree, and the remaining 30 percent had accumulated enough dual-enrollment credits to help them start college with an academic advantage. The school predicts that 85 percent of the 2015 senior class will graduate with AA degrees.

Quest faculty acknowledged the toll it takes to wear so many hats in this small school, where they must constantly be available to students. Yet in 2014, sixteen of the nineteen faculty at Quest had worked at the school for six years or more, and four had been there for twenty years. Just like their students, they remarked, staff who join Quest come prepared to work harder than they ever have before. "We believe in a growth mind-set every bit as much as our students," said Ginna Grimes, one of the school's twenty-year veterans.

The same supports that buoy students also sustain the staff. To be successful at Quest, faculty members concurred, they needed to be experts in their subjects, to care deeply about kids, to be flexible, and to be able to learn from mistakes. But without the intense collegial support they counted on, even these ingredients would not have been enough, they added.

"I guess you'd say we are a family, too," said Grimes.

A Complicated Bargain

Dual enrollment has sharpened Quest's focus on ambitious learning. It has deepened the school's commitment to students for whom low family income seemed a barrier to advancement. It has won favor with students and parents alike.

"Graduating from high school with an associate's degree, tuition-free, *plus* a high school diploma—it can't be beat," said one Quest parent. "I know for my son, it puts a shine on all the hard work. He may still be short for his age, but he's got tall dreams."

And for the first time in more than a decade, QECHS is not fighting for its existence with the local school board, which, as noted earlier, has often fretted about the school's size and pedagogy and whose members have become more conservative in recent years. Indeed, in the winter of 2015, the board unanimously "approved" Quest's early college program.

It has been a complicated bargain, however, introducing chinks in the school's hard-won sense of community and its embrace of students learning at their own pace.

Most of Quest's juniors and seniors now spend four days a week taking college courses at the Kingwood Campus of Lone Star Community College, a twenty-minute drive away from the Atascocita Center where the high school resides. The exigencies of transportation mean that these eleventh and twelfth graders usually spend the day at Kingwood, not at Quest. Two mornings a week, they check in at Quest and receive some of the support that once filled their school day, but all agree it is a modest replacement. When college classes are not in session but Quest is, "we get the delicious opportunity to be part of the Quest community again," senior Melissa said.

In addition, the family structure—which formerly brought all four grades together every day—had relied on eleventh and twelfth graders to mentor younger students, to bring their accrued wisdom to family discussions, and to lead activities. Facilitator Jim Nerad called their absence a "phenomenal loss," although ninth grader Amadeus, who never experienced the prior arrangement, gave family "a total thumbs up for helping us grow."

Finally, the expectation that virtually all of Quest students will graduate with an associate's degree (few early college high schools nationwide have set such an ambitious goal) has placed unprecedented pressure on students and facilitators. Students actually start college classes their freshmen year, in dual-credit courses taught by Quest facilitators. The four years that Quest students once had in which to season as adolescent learners—with time and room to learn from failure—are now compressed.

In the fall of 2013, the school created a program for students most at risk of failing, starting with seven tenth graders who seemed unlikely to succeed in college courses starting the next year. Working with Quest's assessment coordinator, Dolly Covington, the students and their parents or guardians drafted individual contracts for how they would address the biggest trouble spots. Each party had a role to play: the school, the student, and the parent. "The goal was to have conversations that got to the root of the problem and gave kids the strategies they needed to be successful, so that they weren't walking around the school feeling they were a failure," said Covington.

In the fall of 2014, when Humble ISD made funds available for "at-risk" coordinators at each high school (along with a list of thirteen factors that placed a student on the at-risk list), Quest split the position between two staff members. By the district's reckoning, at the end of the first quarter, over one hundred Quest students, almost a third of the school, had qualified as at risk. (Some students had brought the at-risk label with them from middle school, an affirmation, if nothing else, that QECHS was not "creaming" for top students.) With that steep and sudden rise in designated at-risk students, Quest began to provide more intensive support to those for whom the school's academic expectations proved a substantial reach. The two at-risk counselors, Saxon Batungbacal and Latonia Thomas Scott, set up a system in which they meet with each student to create a learning plan and then continue to meet weekly with the student to monitor progress and troubleshoot.

Complying with District Mandates

An aberrant in the Humble school district in terms of its educational design, Quest had for two decades managed to go its own way, although it often fought for its existence with local naysayers. "Maybe we lacked the right elevator speech," one veteran staff member said, "but the truth is that the chasm between the community's and our beliefs about teaching and learning has always been huge."

In this back and forth, grades have consistently caused the flash points. Since the district regards GPAs as the primary indicator of success or failure, Quest has always ruffled feathers with its system of using performances and exhibitions assessed by rubrics in place of traditional final exams and grades. With great reluctance, in 2013, the school agreed to adopt the GPA (and class ranks) as a measure of academic achievement, while still holding onto performance assessments when possible. Facilitators turned in grades to the district at the end of each semester.

With the start of the 2014–2015 school year, however, the district began requiring Quest facilitators to turn in grades every nine weeks (a timetable other high schools in the district were already following). The mandate also spelled out the elements that must determine quarterly grades: six formative assignments, four summative assignments, and a final exam (counting for 20 percent of the grade). For Quest, this was a direct challenge to its foundational value of mastery learning, a system that above all honored the time it took for individual students to master difficult content.

At the time of our return visit to Quest in December 2014, staff members were just beginning to sort out the consequences of this new mandate—and the degrees of freedom that remained for them to respond respectfully, but on their own terms.

"I get accountability; I'm all for it," said principal Ginger Noyes. "But when it comes to the complex dynamic of teaching and learning, 'one size fits all' misses the mark. We need an assessment system that's as robust as can be, one that rewards students for their resiliency and models the understanding we try to cultivate in our students."

Adding It Up

After all these years, it would appear that Quest has won the argument: big is not always better. For the first time, the school is turning heads for its top rank, not for its far-out ideas.

Getting there has taken a fierce determination on the part of Quest staff to balance support for ambitious learning with commitment to "whole child" development. "We still manage to be what we've always been," said Noyes. "We are a school that cares deeply about the minds *and* the hearts of every student who enters our doors. But it's an ongoing challenge. It never gets easier."

Along with Quest's surging reputation, its enrollment has risen markedly in the past five years (from 220 in 2010 to at least 356 in 2015). The school has now outgrown its quarters at the Atascocita Center; for some time, Quest has actually had to vacate the building at 4:30 p.m. so as to accommodate Atascocita's needs. It hopes to relocate completely to the larger Kingwood campus of Lone Star Community College, solving the transportation problem that makes it so hard for juniors and seniors taking college courses to remain a part of daily life at Quest. Presumably, those students could also retake their place in the Quest family groups that nurtured them, and mentor the younger peers who follow in their footsteps.

Securing for Quest students the computers and college textbooks they need for college studies has also become a scramble, which entails not just fundraising but also getting books and laptops to students before their college classes start.

However, perhaps the largest challenge Quest now faces is maintaining its autonomy in the face of well-intentioned district mandates. Forms, protocols, and professional development workshops—typically aligned with the circumstances of Humble's five large comprehensive high schools—rarely make sense at Quest. The school must keep, in effect, two ledgers: one for the district; another finely tuned to its own concerns, questions, and data needs. Nowhere is this mismatch greater than in relation to the requirement that schools submit student grades every nine weeks; it strikes at Quest's core belief in mastery learning.

"One of the things I've learned here is that resilience and success go hand in hand," said Melissa who will graduate in 2015 with an associate's degree, the first in her family to attend college. It is a lesson the staff at Quest Early College High School knows well.

EXHIBIT 3.1   APPLICATION TO QUEST EARLY COLLEGE HIGH SCHOOL

Student response required: Please answer the following questions neatly in your own handwriting.

(1) Please check the appropriate box for the following (your answers will not determine acceptance):

     a. Do you use a planner to keep yourself organized?   YES   NO

     b. Are you willing to stay at Quest ECHS for at least one full school year?   YES   NO

     c. Are you capable of challenging school work?   YES   NO

     d. Are you willing to do two to three hours of homework each evening?   YES   NO

     e. Do you feel you have an adequate place to study?   YES   NO

     f. Do you have access to the appropriate school supplies?   YES   NO

(2) If one of your friends asked you to explain why you want to attend Quest Early College High School, what would you tell him/her? Please be specific.

(3) What do you want your high school experience to include? Describe the perfect high school for you to be successful.

(4) An early college high school offers/requires coursework that is a combination of both high school and college courses in a college setting. Explain why you feel prepared to handle this type of educational experience.

Courtesy of QECHS

EXHIBIT 3.2   SERVICE-LEARNING SELF-EVALUATION, QUEST ECHS

(Please complete both pages)

QUEST STUDENT _____

GRADE _____   QECHS FAMILY _____

SERVICE PARTNER _____

SERVICE SITE _____

What service or services did you provide and how did you grow this year:

_____

_____

_____

_____ .

5	4	3	2
E–Excellent	VG–Very Good	S–Satisfactory	N–Needs Improvement

(Circle the appropriate letter)

Attendance/Punctuality:				
I was consistent in attendance	E	VG	S	N
I reported to my site on time	E	VG	S	N
Attitude:				
I accepted responsibility	E	VG	S	N
I dressed appropriately	E	VG	S	N
I was courteous and cooperative	E	VG	S	N
I displayed emotional maturity	E	VG	S	N
I exercised good judgment	E	VG	S	N
I was committed and caring	E	VG	S	N
I interacted appropriately	E	VG	S	N

EXHIBIT 3.2 *(continued)*

5	4	3	2
E–Excellent	VG–Very Good	S–Satisfactory	N–Needs Improvement

(Circle the appropriate letter)

Learning Process:	E	VG	S	N
I showed initiative	E	VG	S	N
I assumed responsibility for my own learning	E	VG	S	N
I demonstrated problem-solving skills	E	VG	S	N
Performance:				
I began work promptly	E	VG	S	N
I handled constructive criticism well	E	VG	S	N
I exhibited competence and confidence	E	VG	S	N
I required little adult supervision	E	VG	S	N
I was a dependable partner	E	VG	S	N

My overall impression of this year's service-learning experience:

_____

_____

_____

_____

_____

**"The best way to find yourself is to lose yourself
in the service of others"—Gandhi**

Thank you for serving your community this year!

Quest Early College High School Staff

EXHIBIT 3.3   PERSUASIVE SPEECH RUBRIC

Speaker _____   Score _____

Topic _____

Criteria	Effectively accomplished		Partially accomplished		Not accomplished	
	5	4	3	2	1	0
Attention Getter	Effective use of attention-getting strategy (quote, statistic, question, story, etc.) to capture listeners' attention and to introduce topic. Attention getter is relevant and meaningful and seemed to gain the desired response from audience.		Use of relevant attention-getting strategy, but did not seem to adequately capture audience attention and/or lead to desired outcome.		No attention-getting strategy was evident. No clear or relevant connection to topic and/or speech purpose.	
Thesis Statement	Speaker clearly formulated and stated thesis statement during the speech introduction. Thesis statement identifies topic and encompasses/previews main points.		Thesis is clearly implied, although not explicitly stated. Topic is clearly identified, but main points are not clearly previewed.		No thesis statement (implied nor explicit). Main points are not clearly identified, audience unsure of direction of the message.	
Connection w/Audience	Clearly stated the relevance of topic to audience needs and interests. Thoughtful audience analysis reflected through choice of topic and supporting evidence.		Topic seems somewhat relevant to audience, but not explicitly stated. Vague reference to audience needs and/or interests.		Topic seems irrelevant to audience needs and interests. No attempt made to connect topic to targeted audience.	

EXHIBIT 3.3 *(continued)*

Criteria	Effectively accomplished 5 4	Partially accomplished 3 2	Not accomplished 1 0
Subject Knowledge	Depth of content reflects knowledge and understanding of topic. Main points adequately substantiated with timely, relevant, and sufficient support. Provided accurate explanation of key concepts.	Provides some support for main points, but needed to elaborate further with explanations, examples, descriptions, etc. Support is relevant, but not timely.	Provides irrelevant or no support. Explanations of concepts are inaccurate or incomplete. Listeners gain little knowledge from presentation.
Organization	Uses effective organizational pattern for speech purpose. Main points are clearly distinguished from supporting details. Signposts are effectively used for smooth and coherent transitions.	General structure/ organization seems adequate but some blurring between main points and supporting details. Logical flow, but no clear signposts for smooth transitions.	Lack of structure. Ideas are not coherent and transitions are forced or blurred. Difficult to identify introduction, body, and conclusion.
Logical appeal	Presents sound arguments to support major claim. Arguments are supported with sufficient, relevant, and valid evidence. Reasoning is free of fallacies.	Some arguments are sufficiently supported but some unsupported assertions are also present. Minor reasoning fallacies.	Arguments lack relevant and valid evidence. Information is incorrect and/or outdated. Many fallacies are present in the reasoning.

Emotional appeal	Effectively and ethically appeals to audience emotions (anger, fear, compassion, etc.) to achieve the persuasive goal. Vivid and emotive language effectively used to create imagery to engage audience emotionally.	Appeals to audience emotions (anger, fear, compassion, etc.) to achieve the persuasive goal, but fails to observe ethical responsibilities. Creates some effective imagery through language.	Fails to appeal to audience emotions. No attempt to use vivid or descriptive language to capture audience emotions.
Credibility	Sources of information (at least three) are clearly identified and properly cited. Establishes credibility and authority of sources presented. Balances a variety of perspectives and recognizes opposing views.	Most sources (less than three) are clearly cited, but fails to effectively establish credibility and authority of sources presented. Seems fair, but fails to acknowledge opposing perspectives.	Fails to identify and cite sources. No attempt is made to establish credibility and authority of sources presented. One-sided argument, no other perspectives are considered. Some identifiable bias.
Eye contact	Consistently and effectively used eye contact to establish rapport with audience. Inconspicuous use of speaker notes and effective use of scanning to establish an expanded zone of interaction.	Conspicuous use of speaker notes. Seems disengaged from audience for noticeable periods of time.	Reads speech from notes/manuscript. Avoids eye contact with audience. Only occasional and sporadic glances.

EXHIBIT 3.3 *(continued)*

Criteria	Effectively accomplished 5 4	Partially accomplished 3 2	Not accomplished 1 0
Body language	Expressive, dynamic, and natural use of gestures, posture, and facial expressions to reinforce and enhance meaning. Body language reflects comfort interacting with audience.	Stiff or unnatural use of nonverbal behaviors. Body language reflects some discomfort interacting with audience. Limited use of gestures to reinforce verbal message.	Body language reflects a reluctance to interact with audience. Distracting movement and/or use of self-adaptive behaviors.
Voice	Natural variation of vocal characteristics (rate, pitch, volume, tone) in Standard English to heighten interest and match message appropriately.	Limited variation of vocal characteristics. Use of rate, pitch, volume, and tone seemed inconsistent at times.	Monotone or inappropriate variation of vocal characteristics. Inconsistent with verbal message.
Fluency	Appropriate pronunciation, enunciation, and articulation. Lack of noticeable vocalized fillers.	Few noticeable errors in pronunciation, enunciation, and articulation. Minimal use of vocalized fillers.	Excessive fluency errors interfered with message comprehension. Excessive use of vocalized fillers.
Professional dress	Appropriate professional attire worn in order to add to credibility.	Appropriate attire worn, though it lacks some professionalism.	Inappropriate attire worn, detracting from credibility.

Total Score _____

Courtesy of QECHS

CHAPTER 4

"We Are Crew, Not Passengers"

Springfield Renaissance School
Springfield, Massachusetts

IDEA AND CONTEXT

It was one of those days at Springfield Renaissance School when every-one was either crying or laughing. People were pouring through the halls, streaming into the big auditorium that Renaissance shares with another district school housed in this sprawling 1990s brick building. This was May 16, the annual Senior Decision Day, and every single twelfth grader was about to stand up before this assembly to announce a postgraduate plan: to each other, to their fellow students in grades six through twelve, and to the teachers and families whose faces shone in the gathered crowd.

Seniors could wear whatever they liked on this day. But so many stu-dents in the audience wore brightly colored college sweatshirts that you wouldn't have known they were also in school uniform, a typical khaki-white-red-black combination that allows exceptions only for apparel bear-ing a college's name. Even some parents were wearing college t-shirts, in this city where manufacturing jobs have dried up, immigration is on the rise, and 78 percent of school-age children live in poverty.

From Renaissance's start in 2006 as a district magnet school, its found-ing principal, Stephen Mahoney, made an explicit commitment to "college acceptance for every graduate." He had good reasons for his optimism. Within fifteen miles of the school lie twenty-five universities and colleges, and the city enjoys a position at the crossroads of New England, where the East–West Route 90 artery intersects the Connecticut River Valley. Despite a stagnant unemployment rate of over 10 percent, its high-tech, medical, and business communities make Springfield the economic center of western Massachusetts. Though its reputation for crime rose dramatically in the past two decades, violence is now declining in a city made famous by its manufacture of guns (at the historic Springfield Armory and at Smith & Wesson). Fame and history generate pride in other areas as well: everyone knows that this is Hoop City, where basketball was invented.

The time was ripe, Mahoney figured, for every Springfield Renaissance graduate to thrive. Starting with a hundred students in grade six and a hundred in grade nine, Renaissance aimed to attract, via an open public lottery, a population reflecting the city's heterogeneity, as federal magnet school guidelines stipulate. In its inclusive classrooms, these students would reach together toward learning goals typically seen in selective schools. They would need robust support—not just in their academic work but also in the social and emotional challenges they faced.

To support the school's ambitious goal, the Renaissance start-up team would need a seasoned partner in school design. It chose to work with Expeditionary Learning (EL), a national school network that began in 1991 as a partnership between progressive educators and Harvard University's Graduate School of Education and now includes more than 160 schools in thirty-one states. The EL design principles and key structures proved a good match for the new school's priorities (see Exhibit 4.1). They offered a well-documented curricular approach, a cadre of experienced coaches, and a focus on social and emotional development in the service of academic excellence.[1]

In the spring of 2013, the students who entered in 2006 as Renaissance's first sixth graders were approaching their high school graduation. Their safe journey—evident in the fact that each student at Senior Decision Day had a viable postsecondary plan in hand—came about with the support of an interlocking system that afforded them structure and guidance, collaboration and autonomy, reflection and public presentation.

A System of Working Parts

To start a school from the ground up resembles architecture in some ways. Imagining its future occupants, one makes fundamental design choices based on dreams and ideals as much as practicalities. *This structure will gather people in. Through this conduit, energy will flow. An opening here will shed light all day long.* Somehow, between the vision and the constructed place, a system of working parts must come together. If its gears turn smoothly—withstanding the battering of everyday use while holding fast to its reason for being—everyone who enters the place can sense it.

Renaissance drew most of its structures and processes from the well-honed resources that Expeditionary Learning had developed over two decades. In the classroom, teachers used Expeditionary Learning protocols to familiarize students with learning targets and to guide inquiry, practice, critique, assessment, and debriefs. Yearly grade-level cross-disciplinary "expeditions" asked students to investigate real-world issues and present their learning before public audiences. Small advisory groups known as "crew" emphasized self-discovery along with curiosity, empathy along with personal responsibility.

Idealistic and progressive, the founding staff began with visions of student-centered classrooms filled with active learning, collaboration, and metacognition. The pioneering sixth and ninth grade classes had their own hopes and dreams, as they chose a school whose student body was both smaller and more heterogeneous than the district norm. Yet as the school's students (and its numbers) grew, those ideals pushed up against reality.

Although starting from scratch offered some advantages, it took several years for Renaissance to establish a climate that reflected and supported its ambitious goals. And while it may seem that the school has it all figured out now, its leaders and staff continue to review and hone their strategies. This chapter investigates and illustrates the choices that Springfield Renaissance School made to help its youth persist and thrive, and what those choices entailed for the adults who helped them on their way.

THE SCHOOL IN ACTION

The Springfield district allows principals some autonomy in choosing staff, but Mahoney had a hard time finding experienced teachers in every field. In addition, many faculty members faced a steep learning curve in carrying out the broad range of academic and social-emotional roles expected of them. To further their professional development, the principal created a full-time position for a lead teacher who would support and advise colleagues in Expeditionary Learning processes: expeditions and investigations, Passage Portfolios, student-led family conferences, advisory crews, exhibitions, standards-based grading, and more.

Mahoney used every means possible to pay teachers for their learning time. He applied grant funds to teacher stipends rather than equipment. He arranged substitutes on days that students took tests, so that teachers could go observe exemplary work in other classrooms and schools with similar demographics. "In concrete, tangible ways, they saw that teaching this way can make their jobs more satisfying," he said. "They heard teachers, kids, and parents describe the change in student engagement."

Renaissance's six-through-twelve design also had a unifying effect on staff development. Teachers reinforced common classroom protocols from year to year as students progressed as a cohort from middle through high school. Collaborative planning achieved even more coherence, Mahoney said, after he asked all eight teaching teams in the school to use a common structure and protocols in their own grade-level and subject-area meetings. He and three other administrators now regularly attend those meetings, to streamline support for the teachers' logistical needs.

Formative Assessment of Academic Behaviors

All Expeditionary Learning schools emphasize clear learning targets, which are regularly assessed in class to yield an ongoing picture of individual students' development. At Renaissance, teachers assess not just subject-area knowledge and skills but also four key habits of work: preparedness, participation, revision, and doing homework (see Exhibit 4.2). They make notes on those student behaviors during class and debrief their observations before the period ends.

In sixth grade, Kayla objected to her teacher watching everything she did, clipboard at the ready. With the support of her adviser, she had realized by eighth grade that "it's not that hard—just do what I need to do." Once in college, explained Sabrina at fifteen, "you're not gonna have these constant reminders of, 'This is what you need to do in class.' So you might as well get into the habit now." As a student named Brianna neared graduation, she reflected that the habits of work had "helped turn me into a better hard worker and a stronger student that is more self-disciplined."

Points earned for habits of work make up a significant part of the grade in every academic subject. Qualifying for the honor roll—which confers such privileges as access to a private bathroom and hosting school visitors—depends entirely on assessments of a student's habits of work.

Schoolwide Reflective Protocols

At regular intervals—during each school year and across the years—students in all Expeditionary Learning schools review and reflect on their work and present it to others. Renaissance students and teachers routinely use common EL protocols for self-assessment, peer critique, and revision.

When Hector, in eleventh grade, chose a forty-hour internship with the principal as his required community service, he was amazed to witness teachers assessing each other's work as rigorously as that of students. "I got to see the way that they used to grade a unit plan," he said. "The way that they really talked about it and they presented their work. And then they would just check off if they met the target or if they didn't. They'll be judged the same way that I was judged in my writing." Indeed, the checklist used to observe teaching at Springfield contains concrete descriptors for the "workshop model" of instruction that teachers are expected to use every day in each class, assessing whether they are promoting higher-order thinking in classroom activities (see Exhibit 4.3).

Renaissance bolsters the habit of reflective review and planning through its student-led conferences, held three times yearly from grades six through twelve. Here again, students follow a common protocol, reviewing their progress with their parents or guardians and their teacher-adviser and setting new goals for both personal and academic growth. "At first it was a little unnerving, but I think as we started doing them a lot more, I feel more confident," said Lauren, in grade eleven. "It really helps me to reflect even when we're not in the process of doing them."

That practice also prepares students for a higher-stakes rite of passage at the end of grades eight and ten. To advance to the next academic tier, at those two points they must present and defend a more encompassing Passage Portfolio of their work before a panel of family members, community guests, teachers, and students.

As Arria Coburn helped her eighth-grade advisee, Jenna, review the binder for her upcoming Passage Portfolio, the two of them talked about the metaphor Jenna had chosen to describe her middle-school years. "I chose the bird, 'cause sometimes I can fly by myself, or I can be with the flock," the girl said. Early on, she had worried about exposing her struggles in math. "In sixth grade I didn't really catch up with the flock. But in seventh grade I did," she explained. "Now I know who I am, I'm not scared to ask for help."

Renaissance has revisited some of its practices as the school has grown. For example, at the suggestion of students, Mahoney and his advisory crew devised and piloted new guidelines for the Passage Portfolio that students must present to a panel of assessors, peers, and family before promotion to grade eleven. That presentation had always included evidence of academic growth, reflections on personal growth and goals, a résumé, and a "credo" statement. The new version, to better match the developmental needs of learners in their mid-teens, added a physical challenge and a service challenge to its requirements, changes that met with enthusiasm across the board.

Committing to Shared Values

If kids aren't happy, "they won't do great," concluded Hector, the eleventh grader who spent forty hours shadowing his principal. "You have to listen to them and know what's going on." That listening began at the very start of Renaissance's first year, when the school asked its initial group of sixth and ninth graders to put words to the leadership qualities they most wanted to see in themselves and others.

"It wasn't just teachers saying, 'This is how it's gonna be run,'" Lauren recalled six years later, in grade eleven. "It was students voicing their opinions and saying what they wanted in the school." Those conversations yielded seven character traits—friendship, perseverance, responsibility, respect, self-discipline, cultural sensitivity, and courage—which youth and adults at Renaissance agreed to adopt as their "community commitments" (see Exhibit 4.4). Students use those traits as reference points when assessing their own progress in family conferences and Passage Portfolios. In a yearly ritual, when seniors announce their future plans at the annual Decision Day ceremony, seven students stand before the audience and give brief talks on how a particular commitment shaped their journeys to graduation.

"Those are the things that make the school," said Justin, fourteen. "The commitments that we made to not downgrade people, but boost them up so they have the same opportunity that we have to learn. The responsibility part, the friendship part, the cultural sensitivity part, they all tie in together."

Displays in classrooms and hallways recognize and celebrate students who demonstrate various community commitments. (One such poster, featuring a photo of a boy wearing a football jersey and a bashful grin, read: "Ju'Wan has courage. 'I try something new, even when I am afraid.' This is the first year that Ju'Wan has played high school football.") Even some teacher lesson plans at Renaissance now include targets for character development as well as for academic learning and habits of work. During a unit on the age of imperialism, for example, William DeVos assessed students not only on their critiques of U.S. foreign policy but also on whether they "encourage the academic success of those around [them]."

In trusting students to speak for themselves about what matters, Renaissance supported their creation of a shared history with values that they clearly feel they own. In 2013, the student body reconfirmed the criteria and original commitments, as recent student signatures attest on two framed documents displayed in the school's main hallway.

Making Small Actions Count

In the school's first years, however, holding students to those commitments proved one of its biggest challenges. "We created a very loving culture for the kids from the start," Mahoney recalled, but that attitude often edged into chaos in classrooms and halls. "Kids were doing some really wonderful things, but it was peaks and valleys with their acting out in class." By the end of year two, morale had fallen among teachers exhausted from managing student behavior. "We didn't have really clear, consistent, universal accountability in the building," the principal said. "We needed to focus on the ability for folks to regulate themselves."

That summer, Mahoney recruited a teacher task force to come up with a new behavior policy he called "Sweat the Small Stuff." Modeled after the "broken-window theory" regarding antisocial behavior, it focused on a half-dozen minor behaviors (such as uniform violations, or cell phones and food in the classroom) that Mahoney believes "eat away at the consistency and the quality of the learning environment." All school adults agreed to consistently impose clear consequences (culminating in detention) for such matters. Within a year, Mahoney said, "We turned the culture" toward order and respect without sacrificing empathy and nurturance. Since then, the staff conducts a yearly review to revise and prioritize its "Small Stuff" shortlist.

Using Restorative Practices

For larger offenses, such as dishonest behavior, the Renaissance response combines clear consequences with a more therapeutic approach. "We try to make sure that the student thinks through, talks through what happened and why it happened and understands its impact on other people, whether it's the family, the classroom, the teacher, or themselves," said Mahoney. "And then there's a consequence."

Although Mahoney has never expelled a student, "I don't have any qualms about making the individual pay so that the group can benefit," he said. Detentions are routinely handled at lunch or after school. For in-school suspensions, however, students go to the school's Reconstruction Center (known as RC) to reflect on their transgression. They write apologies to their families and those harmed, as well as an essay based on their community commitments. Graver offenses sometimes receive out-of-school suspensions, which involve both making restitution and keeping up with schoolwork. "Every time we do a suspension, there's two audiences: the kid, and then all the other kids and the rest of the community," Mahoney said. "They need to know."

According to students, the message comes through loud and clear. "You never see fights in this school," said Anthony, sixteen. At fifteen Kendra could still recall her first disciplinary incident in middle school, after she slapped a boy with a piece of braided gimp. At that age, "you didn't really know how to control your anger," she explained. "You just thought, 'I'ma just do it and get away with it.'" When the assistant principal took her to RC, Kendra had to write an apology letter to the boy and another to her mother. "You didn't get away with it," she said. "They made sure your parents saw. You got a phone call home, a letter home that day." Ever since, she said, "I'm like, 'I'm never doing this again.'"

Building Relationships in Crew

That focus on maintaining order and respect can succeed largely because the school prioritizes knowing every student well, Mahoney said. (He studies a roster with student names and photos in his free time.) All Renaissance students belong to an advisory group called crew (from the slogan "We are crew, not passengers"). An adult adviser stays with the same group of twelve to fifteen students from grade six through nine; for the high school years, students join a new crew.

Meeting daily during first period, crew is a credit-bearing class complete with learning targets and assessments; its curriculum combines social-emotional development with academic goal setting, advisement, and support. College planning and career exploration take place in crew, as do community service and challenge activities such as the Outward Bound expedition. Crew is so important that teachers use a common checklist to make sure they are hitting all its expected goals (see Exhibit 4.5).

The sustained relationships built in the "crew family" forge close bonds of trust, by all accounts. Although students may have their crew teacher for an academic class as well, "it's a very different relationship," said Lauren, in grade eleven. "They get to know you in a different way than they do in the classroom." Peer relationships also grow stronger, she added. "Being together for so long, the people really get to know each other and everyone kind of has each other's backs."

Dustin, a tenth grader, described his school days as filled with emotional ups and downs. "My crew teacher is kinda like a second mom to me," he said. "Having that one person that you know is always gonna be your friend is really good."

Navigating Troubled Waters

Teachers in academic classes, students reported, also care about their well-being. "They take their time and you can tell that they care," said Sabrina, fifteen. "They're not just here for a job." Kayla declared in eighth grade that her teachers were "willing to make ways for you to do your best. If that means that if they need to come earlier in the morning to help you, they will do that. If they need to stay after school hours, they will do that. You always have somebody that you can lean on."

"The academics and the emotions and the socialness, it really does all mesh together," said Dustin. "If you don't feel happy, then you're just gonna sit there and kind of give attitude to the teacher."

Despite the relationships Renaissance teachers build in the service of learning, however, they do not have the time or training to serve as mental health counselors. The school's well-staffed guidance office keeps classroom management issues from escalating, helping students regain their emotional balance without disrupting class.

Three full-time members of the guidance staff (two for social-emotional matters, one for college counseling) work from a spacious suite of rooms ideal for individual as well as small group sessions. They get valuable reinforcement from six to nine graduate students in social work from Smith, Mount Holyoke, University of Massachusetts in Amherst, and Springfield College, who serve as interns (most of them full time) for most of the school year.

Anthony, at fifteen, had seen his share of days when "I can't even show my face in class," he confided, because of "those things that pump you up and it gets you mad or it gets you down." After even just a short time in the guidance office, he could return to class and "hop right in it," he said. In ninth grade, Justin felt more safe acknowledging a problem when the whole class was not "just stopping and focusing on you," he said. "Because that sometimes can be overwhelming."

Teachers especially appreciate the support. Jessica Engebretson recalled a student in her seventh-grade science class for whom the school provided regular counseling in anger management. In time, she said, he could identify when he was getting upset and ask for space, going into the hallway or making a brief visit to the guidance office and coming back calmer. Engebretson, too, learned to recognize his signals and suggest a break. Over the year she saw his academic work improve, she said. Even better, "this understanding between us built a rapport that is still growing in his eighth-grade year."

Putting Families in the Picture

Family members are highly visible members of the Renaissance community. "They always bring family in," said Kayla in eighth grade, describing a recent Exhibition Night and potluck family dinner. "I guess other parents talk to each other when we have these kind of things, and they get to know your families. They want your family to come in and see, 'Oh, this is what my child is doing,' or 'This is what her peers are doing.'"

Nowhere is this connection more evident than in the family conferences everyone calls "student-leds." For several days in late fall, winter, and spring, in virtually every nook and corner of the school, one sees small groups of chairs where students are presenting their progress to parents or guardians, in the company of their crew teacher.

Students must take the lead throughout the conference, working with their families and crew teacher to set or keep SMART goals (so called because they are specific, measurable, attainable, relevant, and timely). Because crew keeps students with the same adviser for several years, these occasions develop into ongoing conversations that foster trust and understanding across generations and roles.

Kayla struggled with procrastination, for example, but she came to see her mother as a model of perseverance (one of the school's community commitments). "She's determined to finish her stuff," Kayla said. "She doesn't let things go in her way. So when I look up to her, like, 'Oh, I wanna be my mom,' I wanna be able to push through that hard stuff."

As Renaissance teachers come to know families better, they find new ways to support students through hard times. In twelfth grade, Brianna looked back on two key periods when her teachers served as an emotional and academic lifeline. The first came just before her transition to ninth grade, when a beloved grandfather died. "My mind wasn't there, and I just wasn't in the right place," she said. "I remember them really being there for me. And it was hard, but they did help me get through it." When, in eleventh grade, Brianna's entire college savings had to go toward the care of her ailing grandmother, the school guidance office went all out to send scholarship opportunities her way. "Even though me and my family have been through so much, they see the potential in me," she said with pride. "I didn't think I was gonna be able to really financially make the task of going to college, but now they've helped make that possible."

Academic Connection and Engagement

Such absorption and commitment could not happen without curriculum that matters to students and to their world, the founders of this school believed. "The idea is to put really important and difficult work together with great joy in doing it," according to Greg Farrell, who founded the Expeditionary Learning Outward Bound schools network in 1990 and still serves as its president emeritus.

To that end, EL schools infuse the curriculum with learning "expeditions"—serious inquiries into challenging cross-disciplinary issues, in which students address the authentic needs of an audience other than their teachers. In an expedition titled "Power, Passion, Peril," eleventh graders read a first-hand account of Hiroshima in English class, studied the dangers and benefits of nuclear materials in chemistry class, and analyzed how nuclear power has shaped history in recent decades. Field trips enlivened the expedition, one student said afterward, offering "a little break from the traditional academics in the traditional classroom." In other yearly expeditions, sixth graders investigate chocolate, seventh graders explore archeology, eighth graders study the physics of roller coasters, ninth graders analyze water quality in the Connecticut River, and tenth graders look into antibiotic-resistant bacteria. Seniors recently took up a new inquiry topic, the "school-to-prison pipeline."

Keeping student work before the public eye carries great importance in the Expeditionary Learning design. The halls of Renaissance bear witness to that with poster displays of what students produce, but the work also travels into the larger community. Case studies, projects, fieldwork, consultation with community experts, and service learning all generate public audiences and raise the stakes for the production and exhibition of high-quality work. For example, Springfield's facilities engineer, Joseph Forest, asked the ninth-grade environmental science class at Renaissance to collect data and make a recommendation for energy conservation in the city's school buildings. Students presented their "Greenprint" to the mayor and, by following their recommendations, the city saved thousands of dollars in energy costs.

Student Choice and Challenge

Having some choice about what and how they learned mattered a lot to these adolescent students, they said. Much of their Renaissance curriculum follows the traditional subject-area progression, and budgetary constraints also limit the range of courses the school can offer. However, teachers have created other ways to build choice into student learning. As Dustin reflected in tenth grade, they "expect the unexpected," looking for and using the positive things that energize students. Even students that "look like they're the bad kids always getting in trouble," he said, can be "really, truly passionate people. You just need to find that trigger that turns on that passion so that they can really show it off in class."

Just before winter and summer vacations, regular classes come to a halt, making room for a week of over three dozen intensive elective courses—largely in athletics and the arts—that build on the particular interests of staff, students, or outside experts. (Among recent offerings: Scrapbooking,

Civil Rights Poetry Slam, Drawing like the Great Masters, and Survival: Who Lives? Who Dies?) The intensives, said Principal Mahoney, turn a week that is "too often wasted watching videos and just hanging out" into valuable experiential learning instead.

In eleventh grade, for example, Lauren took the opportunity to learn to flip a kayak in the school's swimming pool. She relished the chance, she said, "to kind of get out of my comfort zone and try something new that was really fun with a group of students who I never really talked to before." Another student started his own soccer intensive, planning and executing the entire week with a teacher as sponsor.

In tenth grade, Anthony got hooked on music production in an intensive called Hip Hop Around the World, which culminated in a CD and a performance for the school. He took the course for two years before it ended and then joined a community program founded by the two artists who had taught it. Writing and producing his own music gave him more satisfaction than anything he had ever done, he said. "Last week I finished this song and I got my parents and my family members together in the living room and said, 'How does this sound?' You know, got feedback on it. It put a smile on my face—you got your family around and you have what you love doing most."

Some intensive courses take up issues that have social and emotional import. For example, in her senior year, Megan, one of the school's founding sixth graders, created an intensive in which students revisited the school's community commitments. In another mini-course, Kayla and a group of eighth-grade classmates looked into the issue of bullying. "We wanted to see where is this happening, where is it coming from, and how we can stop it," she said. "One way was creating social networks about bullying. If you do say something to someone, make it in a positive way."

Expeditions and Service

Although EL's initial formal partnership with Outward Bound has largely concluded, outdoor and wilderness expeditions also play a signature role at many of its schools. Every fall the Renaissance ninth-grade class (and some transfer sophomores) participate in a week-long Outward Bound course, hiking in the mountains of Maine. The resulting social and emotional benefits carry over into academics, Principal Mahoney noted, and students agreed. "It was scary at first. I wanted to quit, and I didn't," said Hector, sixteen. "After that I got to see who was I as a real person. Now I really know what I can do and what I cannot do."

Exceptionally diverse in its demographics as well as its business and cultural institutions, the Springfield area affords many opportunities for the community service that Renaissance considers fundamental to adolescent education. All students complete forty hours of service before graduation, and crew teachers as well as administrative and counseling staff pitch in to help with the logistics involved.

At its start, the school earned a reputation for service, recalled Megan in her senior year. But in the push to become "academically notable," she said, that priority drew less emphasis. Before they graduate, Renaissance seniors create farewell "legacy projects"; as hers, Megan helped organize a community run for local charities. "I just want to leave a mark somehow," she said, "and to get our students out into the community."

Throughout middle school, Kendra belonged to a girls service-learning group called "Ladies of Elegance," which focused on building confidence, poise, and self-respect in early adolescence. Reluctant at first, she found herself coming out of her shell as the girls interacted with other young people in the community. "I actually did a room over, at a teen shelter for young ladies who have babies," she said. "And it really helped out with not only myself, but with others."

Such community connections stoke the fires of learning and can lead to serious thoughts about future careers. Ever since middle school Jesse participated in school governance, and in eleventh grade he found an internship with a local political organization. By senior year, he had worked on campaigns for the city council and state senate. "I've really started building a political career in Springfield already," he said. "But I was able to really learn all these skills in a more small community that really took me seriously 'cause I was a student at the school."

Taking Positive Risks

Approaching the end of his tenth-grade year, Dustin spoke willingly about the social challenges of adolescence. "Everyone has their secrets," he said, his eyes humorous behind black-framed glasses in an ample face. "You can't just express it out there, because you might cause some drama. Then people start spreading rumors and that just adds even more stress." Recalling his experience in sixth and seventh grades, he said, "I would be the last one to be picked for a group."

Since then, he said, things have changed. "All of us have really learned to mingle and really interact with each other. Like learned what not to say, what to say, how to not push the buttons, how to not pull strings, really tell if someone's annoyed or not." At sixteen, "there are times when I do feel like an outsider," Dustin said. "But then something else happens and I feel in again."

Such a shift had recently happened, as Dustin assembled the Passage Portfolio that would demonstrate his readiness for the last two years of high school. As part of its requirements, he explained, "I had to do a physical challenge, and I'm not really that athletic." But he had always loved to dance. Aware that he was crossing traditional gender roles, Dustin tried out for cheerleading. He made the team, the first male ever to do so.

In another school, Dustin said, "People would've probably started talking like, you know, crap about me." But finally he had found a team sport that he could envision continuing for years to come. He had already started to choreograph the cheerleading routines, and was imagining studying business management in college and eventually opening his own dance studio. For these positive developments, Dustin credited "this environment, this atmosphere" at Renaissance. "You really feel that you can be successful in anything," he said.

Nicholas, an eighth grader, had also started to experiment with possible selves. "Some students feel very comfortable talking about their real self," he said. "But students like me, I put on a very different mask when I'm at school." Though others may consider him happy and outgoing, he declared, "I'm not like that, other places. I'm very quiet. I'm reserved, and I don't, I don't like to stand out." In Nicholas's view, his school "gives you a place to not be something you're not, but to be something better than you are . . . without being fake, essentially." During a Spirit Week the previous year, he tried dressing for school completely in orange to signal his individualistic bent. "I won Spirit King that week," he said with satisfaction. "If I hadn't felt so comfortable with the people I was around to show my real self, maybe I wouldn't have done that."

Forming an Identity

Bridget Camara teaches the drama course that all Renaissance students take for a semester in grades nine, ten, and twelve. (Eleventh graders must take a semester of health instead.) Its chief point, she said, is not to learn to act but rather "to find your voice." Starting with scenes from their own lives, Camara aims to help even the most introverted of youth "at least get up there and say something," she said. For the extroverts, "it's about trying to learn to listen to other people and try to have some self-control," she noted. "But then also [to] have the discipline to make your performance for an audience, not just for your own benefit."

Anthony wished he had even more opportunities for creative expression in his tenth-grade academic classes. Still, he had recently brought his passion for hip hop into an English class writing assignment called "I Am." It took him five hours to write those hundred lines, he said. "There's a lot of things that people don't know about me from school—even though they have been with me since sixth grade—that I'd like them to finally realize. So I took the time to make a big plot. This is who I am. This is what I want people to know about me."

Many other students spoke of pivotal school experiences that supported their search for identity. To a striking extent, these situations had also persuaded them that their own effort, not talent, was increasing their ability and competence.[2]

By the end of tenth grade, for example, Hector saw himself as someone who could "take on challenges that not everyone will take." He said, "Courage means to confront your fears, keep it going even though it's hard. And that's what I'm basically known for here at my school." Despite his apprehension about sports, Hector had tried out for the swim team to fulfill the physical challenge requirement for his Passage Portfolio. Success at that gave him the confidence to try baseball later in the year. "I can look at myself in the mirror now," he said with satisfaction, "and definitely say who am I as a person."

When her crew advisory planned a class meeting for the whole ninth grade, Sabrina also felt her courage tested. "It's hard for me to get up on stage and talk to a group of one hundred students, because it's something that I never did before," she said. But she felt that "I need to take part in this. I need to make sure this goes well with my crew. I was kind of like one of the main people planning. . . . I need to work hard on it."

As she approached high school graduation, Brianna too reflected on her development from a hesitant sixth grader into a leader. "Going through seventh and eighth grade, I was still trying to come out of my shyness," she said. Then the school's annual Outward Bound wilderness expedition for rising ninth graders challenged her to try a different role ("like leading my group through the forest at one o'clock in the morning, just to get to our next campsite"). Brianna considers that experience "one of the hardest times in my life. I cried, like, every day." Still, she believes that it also made her stronger. "I kinda call my transformation from sixth to twelfth grade like a butterfly kind of like coming out of its cocoon," she said. "Like getting ready to fly and going on to college and having to spread my wings there."

Belonging to a Community

"I'm not from what you would call maybe the best neighborhood," Justin said at fourteen, adding that he often chooses to stick around at the end of the day rather than get on the bus home. The mutual trust built up in his crew advisory group gave him a safe base of belonging from which he soon began to branch out. "There's people here that they're easy to talk to," he said. "It's not like a setting where you have to limit yourself." Though he recognized the differences among his peers, Justin did not see exclusion as an issue. "We all try to be friends, even if something's not working out that good," he said. "You're not gonna love everybody, but the, just, respect that we have for each other—not to disrespect each other—it really helps everybody be comfortable with saying what they feel."

In eleventh grade, Hector recalled what it was like for him as a new sixth grader and an English language learner. In his previous school, he had adopted a "protective mode," and when he arrived at Renaissance, "I did not even know how to introduce myself." Using team-building games and other activities, he said, his new school taught him "how to do this friendship-bond thing." Later, Hector made a point of talking to new students and helping them out. "Here is more of a safe environment, and you feel like you're at home more," he said. "I can walk around and it don't matter who's around me. If I turn around, I know who's that person."

Working on the yearbook in ninth grade made Sabrina feel connected to teachers and students throughout the school. "People say, 'Oh, that's a nerdy thing to do,' but I love it," she said, explaining in animated detail why "it's a good thing to be part of." As she and a friend worked on their section, they gathered evidence of student and teacher life both in and out of school: sports, field trips, baby pictures, traditions, the various elements that created community from a very diverse group. "Getting to see their pictures and their stories make it into the yearbook, that's a really big thing," Sabrina declared. "And the yearbook, it just brings everyone together. It symbolizes the school as one."

Describing their interdependency in such ways, these young people revealed the crucial sense of belonging that a large body of research establishes as a key social and emotional foundation for learning.[3] The attachments they describe are fertilizing the soil for their developing sense of identity, competence, autonomy, and agency.[4]

Growing into Something Bigger

"We do put a lot of emphasis on planning here," Nicholas commented, as his ninth-grade year drew to a close. His teachers "never let us just jump into work," he said. "It's always, 'You need to plan out what steps you're going to do. Make sure you have what you need to do to fill out those steps. And then complete the steps.'" After his science class studied the engineering design process, teachers of other subjects also adopted it—"because it fits!" Nicholas explained. "Finding out the question, finding out possible solutions, doing the possible solutions, picking out the best one. And then redoing the process again until you find the best answer."

In eighth grade, Kayla aspired to be a coroner like those she saw on television's *CSI* series. She pushed herself to do better in science classes, where she had often struggled. "I feel like I'm getting better as I study more and I do more work or I ask peers for help," she said. "I wanna push myself to be better." In a seventh-grade crew session on looking ahead to college, she discovered that New York University offered "a really big forensic science major, where coroners would come in, too." Kayla immediately put NYU on her dream list of colleges and also began researching other institutions with forensics programs.

"Success is within me," Dustin declared after he spoke with his tenth-grade teachers about the possibility of taking honors and Advanced Placement classes the following year. Though once he had thought that impossible, now he realized that stretching toward difficult work "really does affect me later on in life," he said. "I may have a goal to get an A in biology, but that A can get me into honors chemistry" and on to AP psychology or physics. The chance to reach higher boosted his self-esteem, helping him "keep going in school and not give up just because of one bad grade," he concluded. "I really want to reach that extra step."

Nicholas could have been speaking for many of his schoolmates as he reflected that his confidence, determination, and perseverance had all increased during his time at Renaissance. "It's you talking, and you need to get comfortable with that," he declared. "And I feel like here is where I learned it from. It allows you to grow into something bigger than yourself."

RESULTS AND SUSTAINABILITY

Despite the familiar challenges of a district school—budget cuts, teacher time, and the like—the gears continue to turn smoothly at Renaissance. We have seen how the school benefited from its access to the curricular, instructional, and assessment resources of the Expeditionary Learning national network, known for its high standards and student-centered practices. As an Expeditionary Learning Mentor School, Renaissance now regularly hosts site seminars for educators from around the country who seek a model of those practices in an urban public middle and high school.

The school's status as a district magnet school gives it an unusually diverse profile in a city with dozens of distinct neighborhoods ranging from rough to rich. Neighborhoods with high populations of school-age children often have higher concentrations of low-income and minority households, as is the case in Springfield. When those children attend racially and economically isolated schools, even with added resources, their academic performance suffers.[5] Federal guidelines for funding magnet schools seek to reverse the ill effects of such patterns by incentivizing school enrollments that instead reflect the overall demographics of the city. In integrated schools, the achievement of such students rises without any harmful effects for their middle-class peers.[6]

Preparing Students for College and Career

Renaissance has thus far steadily met its paramount goal: that every student graduate and gain acceptance to college. Fifteen percent of those actually begin their college studies early, through dual-enrollment opportunities at nearby colleges and universities. Thirty-seven percent of Renaissance students enroll in honors and Advanced Placement courses, and the school's graduating seniors have earned more than $2 million in scholarship offers each year.

Once its students entered college, the pioneering class of 2010 at Renaissance strikingly outperformed its Springfield peers. From 28 to 32 percent of the first cohort of Renaissance graduates finished college in four years; the school expects 45 to 50 percent to have matriculated in six years. In contrast, only 8 percent of Springfield high school graduates achieve college graduation within six years.

In each racial or ethnic category, Renaissance students consistently achieve the best scores in their district on the highly regarded Massachusetts Comprehensive Assessment System (MCAS) tests. Similarly, low-income students at Renaissance (59.7 percent of those enrolled) significantly outperform other low-income students districtwide (85.6 percent).

Self-selection bias may have resulted in the relatively low proportion of Renaissance students with learning disabilities (10.9 percent, compared to 20.7 in the district overall). Yet 20 to 30 percent of students who arrive with individual education plans (IEPs) transition from that category at Renaissance; the remainder consistently show better academic outcomes than those with disabilities elsewhere in the district.

Standardized tests aside, the Springfield community bears continual witness to the high quality of work that Renaissance students achieve. Case studies, projects, fieldwork, consultation with community experts, and service learning all generate public audiences and raise the stakes for the production and exhibition of high-quality work.

Supporting Teacher Leadership

Strong and committed leadership plays a large part in the school's success. Principal Mahoney put down roots in Springfield when he moved his family from California to start the school where his three sons enrolled. Nine years later, he often bicycled to work and took pride that 90 percent of his staff have earned "highly qualified" status. Their expertise also makes them attractive to other districts; teacher attrition at Renaissance amounts to between 10 and 15 percent yearly. However, no teacher who has left Renaissance has also left the teaching profession, Mahoney noted, and seven of its former teachers now work as school designers or school leaders elsewhere. As this volume went to press, Mahoney himself concluded his tenth and final year at Springfield, taking a position at the Harvard University Graduate School of Education where he will create a new national program of teacher training.

As a laboratory school, Renaissance also plays a part in preparing future educators. Each year more than sixty interns prepare for certification in the fields of clinical counseling or teaching by working at Renaissance, and twelve of the school's forty teachers began as interns there.

Renaissance has a key advantage in the Expeditionary Learning network, which served at once as research base and resource bank to the new school as it grew. With its sights set on bringing its approach to scale, EL uses open-source technology to provide abundant exemplars of curriculum and instructional practices, assessment protocols, videos of teachers at work, and, most crucially, actual student work. Although its member schools have deeper levels of access and coaching, much of that material is freely available online.

Renaissance now acts as a mentor school for other Expeditionary Learning schools. Its teachers regularly present at national conferences; many have also won recognition for teacher excellence in awards from the state, the city, and the Harold Grinspoon Foundation. The school receives three to four hundred visitors every year, from near and far. In 2013, Mahoney was honored as Magnet School Principal of the Year for the New England region. Massachusetts has named Renaissance a Commonwealth Innovation School; in 2011, 2013, and 2014, it also won a Magnet Schools of Excellence Award; and 21st Century Schools selected it as one of two hundred exemplary schools around the nation.

Owning the Journey

This school sometimes came across as too good to be true. Its adolescents presented their experience in fervent positives, even when speaking of serious academic or emotional difficulties. They rattled off their community commitments and habits of work like a chant ingrained in some long-ago boot camp. Yet in most ways their school was full of the normal trials of a typical American high school. Definitely, kids here got into trouble and went to detention. Certainly, teachers complained of not enough time for all they had to do. What force had outweighed these things and instilled such a schoolwide culture of cooperation?

The answer seems to lie in the school's thoroughly developmental outlook toward students and adults alike. As Renaissance students advance from the middle grades through high school, one can see and hear them taking ownership of their learning, finding their own voices, considering their own values, charting their own courses.[7] With adults as guides, they grow to believe that success is possible and within their control, acquiring the sense of agency that leads to a productive and satisfying life.

Teachers and school leaders also had a developmental process to go through, as they created a start-up district school with an idealistic vision of diversity and universal college readiness. They managed it by scaffolding their own learning every step of the way, with the steadying force of the Expeditionary Learning network at their backs. As they adopted and adapted a "system of working parts" during the school's first nine years, they continually assessed their progress and grew in self-knowledge and agency, just as they were asking students to do. Like the adolescents whom it serves, Springfield Renaissance has clearly owned every step of the journey toward maturity.

EXHIBIT 4.1   EXPEDITIONARY LEARNING DESIGN PRINCIPLES

Expeditionary Learning is built on ten design principles that reflect the educational values and beliefs of Kurt Hahn, founder of Outward Bound. These principles animate our research-based model for transforming teaching, learning, and the culture of schools.

1. THE PRIMACY OF SELF-DISCOVERY

Learning happens best with emotion, challenge, and the requisite support. People discover their abilities, values, passions, and responsibilities in situations that offer adventure and the unexpected. In Expeditionary Learning schools, students undertake tasks that require perseverance, fitness, craftsmanship, imagination, self-discipline, and significant achievement. A teacher's primary task is to help students overcome their fears and discover they can do more than they think they can.

2. THE HAVING OF WONDERFUL IDEAS

Teaching in Expeditionary Learning schools fosters curiosity about the world by creating learning situations that provide something important to think about, time to experiment, and time to make sense of what is observed.

3. THE RESPONSIBILITY FOR LEARNING

Learning is both a personal process of discovery and a social activity. Everyone learns both individually and as part of a group. Every aspect of an Expeditionary Learning school encourages both children and adults to become increasingly responsible for directing their own personal and collective learning.

4. EMPATHY AND CARING

Learning is fostered best in communities where students' and teachers' ideas are respected and where there is mutual trust. Learning groups are small in Expeditionary Learning schools, with a caring adult looking after the progress and acting as an advocate for each child. Older students mentor younger ones, and students feel physically and emotionally safe.

5. SUCCESS AND FAILURE

All students need to be successful if they are to build the confidence and capacity to take risks and meet increasingly difficult challenges. But it is also important for students to learn from their failures, to persevere when things are hard, and to learn to turn disabilities into opportunities.

EXHIBIT 4.1   *(continued)*

6. COLLABORATION AND COMPETITION

Individual development and group development are integrated so that the value of friendship, trust, and group action is clear. Students are encouraged to compete, not against each other, but with their own personal best and with rigorous standards of excellence.

7. DIVERSITY AND INCLUSION

Both diversity and inclusion increase the richness of ideas, creative power, problem-solving ability, and respect for others. In Expeditionary Learning schools, students investigate and value their different histories and talents as well as those of other communities and cultures. Schools and learning groups are heterogeneous.

8. THE NATURAL WORLD

A direct and respectful relationship with the natural world refreshes the human spirit and teaches the important ideas of recurring cycles and cause and effect. Students learn to become stewards of the earth and of future generations.

9. SOLITUDE AND REFLECTION

Students and teachers need time alone to explore their own thoughts, make their own connections, and create their own ideas. They also need to exchange their reflections with other students and with adults.

10. SERVICE AND COMPASSION

We are crew, not passengers. Students and teachers are strengthened by acts of consequential service to others, and one of an Expeditionary Learning school's primary functions is to prepare students with the attitudes and skills to learn from and be of service.

EXHIBIT 4.2   HABITS OF WORK RUBRIC

Habit of work 1: I come to class ready to learn.

Assessed by:

50% = I come to class on time.

Using the scoring rubric directly below.

Rubric

		For example, in a 40-day period
4 = 97–100% on time	2 = 82–91% on time	0–1 time late
3 = 92–96% on time	1 = below 82% on time	2–3 times late
		4–7 times late
		>7 times late

50% = I have my materials on my desk. I am immediately on task and working hard.

Using the rubric directly below; must be recorded at least 8 times each quarter.

4	3	2	1
• I am meeting the criteria for a 3. AND • I work silently, unless asked by the teacher to talk.	• I have all required materials on my desk. • I write my homework in my agenda book. • I begin my Do Now right away. • I work on my Do Now until I am finished. • I get distracted occasionally during the Do Now time.	• I have most of my materials. • I do not write my homework in my agenda book. • I arrive late at my seat. • I begin my Do Now late. • I complete most of my Do Now. • I get distracted several times during the Do Now time.	• I am missing several materials. • I complete very little of my Do Now. • I make it difficult for other people to focus on their Do Now.

EXHIBIT 4.2   *(continued)*

Habit of work 2: I actively and collaboratively participate in class.

Assessed by:

Using the rubric directly below; must be recorded at least 8 times each quarter.

4	3	2	1
• I am meeting the criteria for a 3. AND • I am asking questions that push my and others' understanding further. AND • I am playing a leadership role in my group by: • Helping keep people on task and focused. • Pushing the group to achieve the goal. • Making sure all voices are heard. • Helping the group come to consensus and/or compromise.	• I am on task. • I am SLANTing: sitting up, leaning in, asking and answering questions, nodding, tracking the speaker. (actively listening) • I am not interrupting or distracting others. • I am respectful to others. • I am doing an equal share of the work. • I am actively contributing and responding to ideas.	• I am on task some of the time. • I know what is going on in class, but I am not participating. • I am not SLANTing consistently. • I am interrupting or distracting others some of the time. • I am somewhat disrespectful to others. • I need some redirection from the teacher or a peer. • I make some contributions to my group but my focus is inconsistent.	• I am not on task. • I am not SLANTing. • I am interrupting or distracting others repeatedly. • I do not respond positively and/or respectfully to others. • I am not contributing to my group.

Habit of work 3: I assess and revise my own work.

Assessed by:

Using the rubric directly below; must be recorded at least 8 times each quarter.

	4	3	2	1
Revision after work is graded (when allowed)	• I earned a 3 or 4 on the assignment the first time and therefore did not feel the need to revise. OR • After receiving a grade, I revised my work using the rubric and feedback AND I achieved a 3 or 4.	• After receiving a grade, I revised my work using the rubric and feedback AND I made significant improvements but did not earn a 3 or 4 on the assessment. • I worked with a teacher so that I better understand the material.	• After receiving a grade, I revised my work but did not seem to use the rubric or make significant changes. • I did not ask for help in order to better understand the material.	• I did not revise my work.
Revision before work is graded	• I am meeting the criteria for a 3. AND • I use all feedback (including from critique, conferencing, and written feedback) to improve my work.	• I use the learning target and rubric to assess, critique, and/or revise. • I show perseverance through the critique and revision process until my work meets the target.	• I do not fully use feedback to revise my work. • My revisions are superficial (surface-level).	• I do not use feedback to revise my work.

EXHIBIT 4.2   *(continued)*

	4	3	2	1
Self-assessment	• I am meeting the criteria for a 3. AND • I analyze my progress in the context of a learning target, rubric, or Quality of a Renaissance Graduate.	• I name learning targets, parts of the rubric, or a Quality of a Renaissance Graduate in my self-assessment. • My self-assessment is accurate, honest, and shows that I am trying to understand my progress and improve.	• I don't put a great deal of thought or effort into assessing myself, but my assessment is somewhat accurate.	• I do not participate in opportunities for self-assessment. OR • My self-assessment is not accurate.

Habit of work 4: I complete daily homework.

Assessed by:

Using the scoring rubric directly below; must be recorded daily.

Rubric	For example, in a 40-day period	For example, in a 20-day period
4 = 90–100% done	36–40 done	18–20 done
3 = 80–89% done	32–35 done	16–17 done
2 = 70–79% done	28–31 done	14–15 done
1 = below 70% done	<28 done	<14 done

Courtesy of Lindsay Slabich and Arria Coburn, EL coordinators at Springfield Renaissance School

EXHIBIT 4.3   TEACHER OBSERVATION CHECKLIST

WORKSHOP MODEL

Learning Targets

Daily Learning Target connected to Semester Learning Target and referenced at least at the beginning (with agenda walk), during, and at end (with debrief).

Do Now

Gets kids on task and subject, timed for teacher admin tasks. Must be work students can handle independently and have a product. *Less than 7 minutes*

Mini-Lesson

Teachers model the work (for example, walking through the work with an explanation or critiquing an exemplar).

Guided Practice

Teachers provide students with an opportunity to practice the skill that was modeled in the mini-lesson with a quick check for understanding.

Application/Independent Practice

Teachers provide students with the opportunity to apply or practice the skill independently.

Catch and Release

Class is pulled together frequently enough to keep students on track and the "catch" activity improves the following work. Teacher and students check in on specific progress and performance, share effective strategies/models, correct common misunderstandings or misdirections, or answer frequent questions or issues. *7–10 minute intervals*

Cold Call

Cold call is used, with cards, and keeps all students alert and engaged. (Cold call could be used as checking for understanding with directions, process, background knowledge, review sessions, probing questions, etc.)

No Opt-Out

Every student who responds to a question with "I don't know" or the wrong answer is required to repeat the correct answer before the class moves on.

EXHIBIT 4.3   *(continued)*

Debrief

The debrief explicitly connects to the learning target. It allows students and teacher to summarize the day's learning, connect to past and/or future work, or evaluate class performance.

Homework

Homework is designed to improve students' mastery learning targets with a product that allows teacher to check student effort and understanding.

HIGHER-ORDER THINKING

Students are using reasoning and critical thinking skills to answer high-level questions.

Engagement

All students are engaged.

Protocols are used.

Engagement has to do with evidence-based discourse regarding texts and essential topics.

Assessment for Learning and Scaffolding

Assessment for Learning scaffolds to the Assessment of Learning in format and content.

Teacher and students assess for progress toward the learning target throughout class.

Teacher makes instructional moves based on data gathered through these Assessments for Learning.

High-Quality Work

Evidence of working toward products that are authentic and demonstrate higher-order thinking and craftsmanship.

Courtesy of Springfield Renaissance School

EXHIBIT 4.4   CHARACTER TRAITS AND COMMUNITY COMMITMENTS

FRIENDSHIP

- I encourage the academic success of those around me.
- I encourage my peers to act responsibly.
- I can give both critical and positive feedback to my peers.
- I am nice, kind, and polite to all members of my community.
- I welcome visitors, new students, new teachers, and staff.
- I am a role model and mentor for my peers.

PERSEVERANCE

- I work to support my peers when we are struggling.
- I go into situations with a positive attitude.
- I meet my goals even through challenges or obstacles.
- I don't quit.
- I learn from failure.

RESPONSIBILITY

- I make no excuses for the tasks I fail to do.
- I hold myself accountable for my actions.
- I am honest.
- I meet all deadlines.
- Once I start something I finish it to the best of my ability.
- I clean up after myself, recycle, and pick up trash in the school.

RESPECT

- I treat all people with a positive attitude, no matter what the situation.
- I stand up for what I believe in.
- I can agree to disagree with people—amicably and politely.
- I take care of my mind, body, and spirit.
- I make eye contact with people when conversing.
- I observe simple courtesies.

SELF-DISCIPLINE

- I control my words and actions in all situations.
- I hold myself to a high standard at all times.

EXHIBIT 4.4 *(continued)*

- I don't talk over other people.
- I listen more than I talk.
- I follow through with goals and responsibilities even when I would rather be doing something else.
- I sweat the small stuff.
- I have a regular routine (time, place, no phone) for completing homework.

CULTURAL SENSITIVITY

- I actively learn about other cultures so as to become more understanding of other customs and beliefs.
- I value race, ethnicity, religion, sexual orientation, and other forms of diversity at my school.
- I hold my peers accountable for being respectful and creating an open and safe environment for people of all cultures.
- I stand up against ignorance and intolerance.
- I work to understand my own cultural identity.
- I am an ally to my peers regardless of our differences.

COURAGE

- I stand up for people who are being picked on and/or disrespected.
- I make the best choices whether or not they are favored by my peers.
- I take academic, personal, and social risks that help me grow.
- I take on the role of leader as needed.
- I try new things with an open mind and empower those around me to do the same.
- I stop confrontations and conflicts as soon as I can.
- I hold my peers accountable for community norms and expectations.

Courtesy of Springfield Renaissance School

EXHIBIT 4.5 CREW TEACHER RESPONSIBILITIES CHECKLIST

The purpose of this checklist is for teachers to use as a reminder of important crew consistencies. It will also be used by administrators and others to track and share feedback with crew teachers.

Teacher: _____   **Observer:** _____

Date Observed	Crew Teacher Checklist	Resources Available for Support (and resource location)	Notes
	DAILY		
	Daily Learning Target and agenda posted		
	Circle up in designated crew area		
	Daily attendance		
	Daily uniform check		
	Student agenda-check—all students must have an agenda and use it daily (recommended to use as Habit of Work #1 grade)	Habits of Work Rubric	
	CURRICULUM AND INSTRUCTION		
	Weekly lesson plans linked to crew Learning Targets		
	Required grade-level crew units (e.g., 10th grade PSAT prep)	Unit and lesson plans (in EL Commons folders*)	

EXHIBIT 4.5 *(continued)*

Date Observed	Crew Teacher Checklist	Resources Available for Support (and resource location)	Notes
	Conferencing with all students based upon need (weekly, bi-weekly, monthly) individually or in groups	Conferencing lesson plan (in EL Commons folder*)	
	Student-led family conference prep, presentation, assessment, and tracking (Passage, internship, senior talk as appropriate)	Outlines, rubrics, and sample crew plans (in EL Commons folders*)	
	ORGANIZATION		
	Crew norms, Learning Targets, and Habits of Work posted	Crew Learning Targets: 1. I contribute to the school community by following our school's mission and community commitments. 2. I am an organized, self-directed and reflective student. 3. I prepare for success in college.	

Regular communication with grade-level academic team regarding student needs and academic and behavioral performance		
Distribute, collect, and track student information handouts (i.e., handbook receipts, emergency contact forms, etc.)		
Maintain crew working folder or binder for each student with both crew assessments and docs and work pulled for student-led family conferences and Passages	Sample binder or folder table of contents (in EL Commons folder*)	
Regular communication with families of crew members; tracked in a communication log		

Courtesy of Springfield Renaissance School

CHAPTER 5

"A School Where No One Gives Up"

Fenger High School Chicago, Illinois

IDEA AND CONTEXT

The stresses of being a young person in one of Chicago's most violent neighborhoods do not trigger the metal detectors at the student entrance to Fenger High School, on the city's South Side. But they erupt in the classrooms and halls of this "turnaround" school, where small transformations distill hope from heartbreak.

Soft-spoken but tough, Brianna thought that her teacher in senior English class was disrespecting her. She had called out to her teacher, who was helping some other students, but the teacher didn't respond. Maybe it was because Brianna hadn't raised her hand. Brianna got mad, got up, and walked toward the door. "What's going on?" the teacher asked.

"I been trying to call you. I need you to come here!" Brianna shot back.

"Whoa. Come on. Step outside," the teacher said, and Brianna complied. But she had already reached a ten on the anger scale, and nothing the teacher said could stop her from feeling wronged. Her shouting soon drew a nearby security guard—at Fenger, security receives special training in de-escalating such situations—but Brianna was on fire. She dropped the F-bomb and landed in the dean's office.

"What's up?" the dean asked, and Brianna looked down and fell silent. Then she explained: she was pregnant and had a lot on her mind. In a zero tolerance school, Brianna would probably have been suspended, regardless of what had shortened her fuse. At Fenger, the dean decided this matter was best resolved through peer jury, a process that had become part of the school's fierce determination to resolve conflicts peacefully.

Within an hour, Brianna, two of her peers, and her teacher were sitting down and sorting out what had happened and how Brianna could have handled matters differently (including raising her hand). Hard feelings eased, the group helped Brianna master the skill of making a genuine apology, a step she was now eager to take. Fifty-two days shy of graduation, Brianna had regained her place in the commencement line and learned a few lessons in what Fenger's peer jurors call "positivity": a mix that includes self-control, positive emotions, and having goals.

For Robert Spicer, who until 2014 oversaw the school's unique blend of peer jury, peace circles, and supportive listening, Brianna's recalibration was all part of a day's work. It also fit squarely into the school's larger mission: healing and challenging students in a community where shelter, food, safety, nurturing relationships, self-esteem, and success were in short supply.

No Place to Send a Child

A cell-phone video showed the attack in grainy but horrifying detail. On September 24, 2009, a Fenger honors student named Derrion Albert was beaten to death on his way home when he got caught up in a large brawl among teenagers from two neighborhoods on Chicago's South Side. The video gained international attention, and President Barack Obama requested that Attorney General Eric Holder and Secretary of Education Arne Duncan visit Chicago to meet with Fenger students and school officials.

Overnight, Fenger became shorthand for the failure and dysfunction that for decades has maintained a stranglehold on many of America's urban schools. It did not matter that—like most school violence incidents that make headlines—the attack occurred outside school. Violent neighborhoods breed violent schools, not the other way around. And it would be hard to imagine a more precarious neighborhood than Roseland, wracked by homicide and gang fights, with almost 20 percent unemployment and a per capita income $10,000 below the rate for Chicago as a whole.

Regardless, the video cemented in public opinion the idea that Fenger High School was no place to send your child.

Some argue that the die had already been cast against Fenger, when several years earlier the Chicago Public Schools (CPS) closed three neighborhood high schools—all designated as failures—within three miles of

Fenger. One of those, Carver Area High School, served children from the Altgeld Gardens public housing project; gangs from Altgeld Gardens were part of the fight that killed Albert. In 2006, a selective-enrollment military academy started up in the shuttered Carver High. Three public charter schools grew from the ashes of Calumet High School, closed in 2007.

A year after the killing, close to 400 students had fled Fenger. Some found seats in neighborhood charter schools, which were eager for new students (and boasted of strict discipline). Most students enrolled in nearby general high schools with better reputations. When Fenger High School began the school year in September 2009, it had 1,190 students. The following September, enrollment had fallen to 784.

The Turnaround

At age thirty-one, Elizabeth Dozier had already gained a reputation within the Chicago Public Schools as a talented and energetic teacher and administrator. She started as Fenger's principal soon after the district designated it as a turnaround school—and just two weeks before the school caught the world's attention as a cauldron of violence.

Academic failure as well as gang fights had long stalked the halls of Fenger, where roughly 98 percent of the students are African American, 96 percent are low income, almost 40 percent are homeless, and the number of students identified with special needs grows each year (from 20 percent in 2010 to 32 percent in 2014). In 2009, a third of the female students were either pregnant or already teenage mothers. The school's 2008–2009 Illinois Report Card showed that fewer than one percent of the school's eleventh graders scored high enough on at least three of the four parts of the ACT to be considered "college-ready." That same year, student attendance stood at 69 percent, and 37 percent of Fenger students were chronically truant. In 2010, Chicago's Office of Performance Management identified Fenger as one of the lowest performing schools in the city.

Restoring order was Principal Dozier's first priority. Outside school and across the city, a new CPS program called Safe Passage hoped to secure the troubled sidewalks that students like Derrion Albert walked on their way to school and back. Inside Fenger, when the hallway free-for-alls got worse, Dozier started handing out suspensions. (Shoving a student or throwing a gang sign got you ten days.) The images on the school's old surveillance cameras were too blurred to identify participants in a fight, so she installed a new camera system connected to the police department, a first for the city's schools. More than thirty security guards and two police officers patrolled Fenger's three floors. Teachers locked their classroom doors after the period began; students excused for the restroom carried bright yellow passes that measured two feet wide.

The clampdown seemed to contradict the aspirational language that accompanied the school's new "turnaround" status. But it had a straightforward rationale, said Dozier: "We needed to secure the most basic conditions for learning, before our students could thrive."

Dozier sat on the district team charged with replacing most of Fenger's teachers. "Turnaround" status requires evaluation and rehiring of teachers; no more than 50 percent of the existing teachers can be rehired. A little more than a year after the new principal arrived, her staff of seventy-seven included only three teachers from pre-turnaround days. Dozier looked for teachers adept at classroom management. They would have to engage students outside the classroom as well as in. They needed a growth mind-set, for themselves as well as their students. Most important, they had to commit to do whatever it took to keep students on track.

The principal made African American staff a top hiring priority, males most of all. In her first year, she recruited twelve teachers and thirty-five nonteaching staff who were African American males. (By comparison, African American men accounted for less than 2 percent of our nation's teachers in 2011.[1]) "In most of our kids' homes, the males are missing: it's mothers, grandmothers, aunts, cousins," Dozier explained. "When they came to school, I wanted our students to see men—not only as security officers, but as teachers, as leaders."

Digging Deeper

Dozier was keenly aware, however, that zero tolerance policies and fresh teachers would not heal the anger and disappointment that Fenger students carried to school each day. She dug deeper. She and her staff launched an ambitious effort to put social and emotional supports for students at the center of Fenger's yet-to-ignite transformation, supported by a $6 million, three-year school improvement grant from the federal government.

Dozier and her colleagues were acting on their belief that rebuilding Fenger by organizing around academic content alone (rigorous curriculum and strong assessments) would not yield the deep changes they sought.

"We've got to stop worrying about the particular plants we are planting, and worry more about the soil," Charles Payne, a University of Chicago professor, cautioned would-be school reformers. If educators can add to the soil the crucial behaviors and supports that allow students to thrive, Payne argued, "then they can shift fundamental outcomes for young people and schools."[2]

Dozier and her colleagues took these words to heart. As noted earlier, they began by turning to the Boys Town Education Model, a school-based intervention strategy that emphasized preventive and proactive approaches to manage student behavior, build relationships, and teach social skills. Boys Town's long experience with at-risk, and often aggressive, youth seemed a good fit with Fenger's students.[3]

Response to Intervention (commonly abbreviated RTI), a multitiered approach to students with learning and behavior needs, quickly emerged as another core ingredient. A by-product of the 2004 federal Individuals with Disabilities Education Act, RTI offered schools a framework to identify students at risk for poor learning outcomes and then assign them to evidence-based interventions calibrated to their needs.[4] At Fenger—where in 2010, 25 percent of the students were categorized as special needs compared to a district rate of 13 percent—a system that organized individualized supports for these students seemed imperative.

Restorative justice was an additional element included in Fenger's embrace of social and emotional learning. It matched the decision by the Chicago Public Schools to allocate its (one year) federal stimulus funds to a program it called Culture of Calm, which privileged and legitimized the restorative justice principles and practices Robert Spicer had begun enacting at Fenger. At troubled urban schools like Fenger, the school-to-prison pipeline was painfully real, and zero tolerance policies had become a propellant rather than a retardant.[5] Restorative justice promised a remedy.

Meanwhile, meeting the emergency needs of Fenger students for shelter, food, clothing, safety, medical care, and sometimes grief counseling became a daily commitment. "First and foremost, we had to make sure that our students were *okay*," said Dozier.

The End of Federal Funds

When the 2012–2013 school year came to a close, the turnaround at Fenger High School had taken hold. In June 2013, Fenger was one of six high schools across the city that had improved most on the indicators CPS tied to college success, including course performance, attendance, academic skills, and good behavior.

Nationally, Fenger was turning heads. Elizabeth Dozier's story and determination figured prominently in Paul Tough's 2012 book *How Children Succeed: Grit, Curiosity, and the Hidden Power of Character.*[6] In the spring of 2013, CNN taped a multipart series called *Chicagoland*, in which Dozier, her staff, and her students emerged as heroes.

Nonetheless, the school's three-year school improvement grant had come to an end.

When Fenger opened for the 2013–2014 school year, it had lost twenty-eight staff positions including teachers, counselors, a dean, and three of the four student advocates, and the hours of the psychologist and social workers had been reduced substantially. It also lost many of its afterschool programs, along with the trips that allowed students to travel beyond their neighborhood, visiting colleges outside Chicago or cultural citadels like New York City.

The 2014–2015 school year opened with an additional crisis. Only 72 of the expected 100 ninth graders showed up in September. The student population at Fenger, over 2,000 strong through the 1980s, now hovered around 350—which meant that the budget, pegged by CPS to student enrollment, would shrink again. Immediately Fenger staff conducted its own door-to-door investigation to understand the dramatic drop in entering first-year students. In a pattern duplicated across Chicago's most blighted neighborhoods, they found that roughly a third of the students who chose not to enroll were using false addresses to attend suburban schools, a third had moved with their family or been shipped to a relative outside the state, and a third had opted to enroll in one of the growing number of nearby charter schools.

Unwilling to sacrifice the professional staff that had provided the social and emotional supports crucial to the school's turnaround, Dozier let go several teachers and one of the deans and hired two new counselors to augment the one remaining counselor. It remains a challenge to fill Robert

Spicer's large shoes after funding ended for his position as "dean of peace building"—even though he trained a corps of staff in restorative justice practices before he left.

"Fenger is a big puzzle," Dozier reflected. "Everyone and everything forms a piece, each plays a part. When you start pulling out pieces, you lose the whole; you lose the holistic approach our students so desperately need."

This chapter traces this school's herculean effort to tend to the hearts and minds of youth—truly left behind—on Chicago's South Side. Much of the documentation captures structures and practices at Fenger in the three-year period of its federal turnaround funding. The last section examines the challenges Fenger has faced after those funds stopped coming.

THE SCHOOL IN ACTION

The sheer scope of what adults at Fenger do with their time presents an object lesson in recognizing the potential of every adolescent learner. Each action they undertake reflects the commitment to respect, develop, and empower youth, no matter how dire their circumstances. That must start with establishing relationships of trust, as the pages that follow illustrate. Then the trajectory continues, as the habits of learning take hold—first in behavioral challenges, then in intellectual ones.

Social and Emotional Triage

"Can I catch a nap?" a lanky, bleary-eyed youth asked, sticking his head into the office of Alejandra Argerich, Fenger's school psychologist from 2010 to 2013. "Of course," Argerich said, rising to show him into a small, secluded room a few steps away. "Just check in with me before you go back to class." It wasn't the first time this young man had sought the quiet and safety of the school's mental health quarters, Argerich explained. Where he lived, domestic violence often rocked the night; some days he just couldn't stay awake in class. "It is better that he come here and replenish for an hour," she said, "than struggle through the whole day, exhausted."

Asked what they like best about Fenger, students point to the feeling that the staff is "there" for them. They talk about the importance of safety in their lives and why they feel safer at Fenger than anywhere else. "It isn't just security and metal detectors and all that stuff, but the supports you get," said Marcus, in twelfth grade. "The staff, they always have your back, wondering how you're doing, asking if you need to talk. You build trust. And when there's trust, there's safety."

With the $6 million three-year school improvement grant awarded to Fenger in 2010 (of which approximately $1.5 million went directly to CPS), Dozier and her colleagues hired a cadre of staff to provide the long-term intensive social and emotional supports students needed: a full-time psychologist, a social worker, two additional counselors with training in therapeutic interventions (bringing the student-to-counselor ratio down from 350:1 to 50:1), and four "student advocates." These last, in an ad hoc position Fenger created, did whatever it took to meet students' basic needs (from a winter coat to a trip to the emergency room), get students to school and on task when there, and intervene in difficult family circumstances. A team drawn from the larger group (called a CARE team within the Chicago Public Schools)[7] met weekly to review the cases of individual students, identifying those who might benefit from group therapy and other intensive supports. When students sought out that help on their own, "it told us how we're doing planting trust," said the assistant principal, Tosha Jones.

Emerging research bolstered Fenger's substantial investment in supporting students' mental health. Learning how to cope with adversity is an important part of healthy development, the research said. Short-lived stress responses can promote growth, but strong, unrelieved activation of the body's stress management system, in the absence of protective adult support, can be poisonous. The unrelenting stress caused by extreme poverty, neglect, or abuse can weaken the architecture of the developing brain, with long-term consequences for learning, behavior, and both physical and mental health.[8]

Now as then, however, social and emotional triage at Fenger begins in the classroom. Teachers do the best they can to engage students left chronically on edge or under water by anger, depression, and isolation. Sometimes the symptoms are hard to detect; other times they flare up with behaviors impossible to ignore, from heated altercations to pervasive sadness. When circumstances get beyond what teachers can handle, they file a request for behavioral health assistance with the CARE team, including a questionnaire that details the student's strengths and difficulties so that the team can match the intervention to the student's particular circumstances (see Exhibit 5.1).

Occasionally, the triage starts in the halls. When anger or conflict reaches a tipping point, the school's security guards, trained in de-escalating students when emotions become raw, are the first to respond. "The students who are hurtin' and quiet, they don't come up on my radar screen," said Keith Connor, head of security at Fenger. "The ones that are hurtin' and angry, we know them pretty well." As the two deans walk the halls, they keep an eye out for students they know are struggling emotionally and try to engage them in conversation so as to take their temperature.

A straightforward philosophy guides Fenger's mental health work with students. "We will reach out to you," said Argerich. "We're not going to tell you what to do, but we're going to try to help you find out what you need and go from there. You're going to teach us things and we're going to do the same for you."

For its anger therapy groups, Fenger's mental health staff relies on the evidence-based Think First program as its protocol.[9] For trauma, it calls upon the proven Cognitive Behavioral Intervention for Trauma in Schools (CBITS) program, which uses cognitive-behavioral techniques to reduce symptoms of post-traumatic stress disorder (PTSD), depression, and behavioral problems in adolescents. Grief counseling is ongoing—a testament to the amount of loss experienced by youth in this community.[10]

Whatever the group, the goals are the same, Argerich said. "We help kids gather their own resources, to find the protective factors they may have but don't know they have—along with the ones they need to learn. And we try to build with them a network of support, here at the school, with friends, with a teacher."

This approach doesn't work every time, Argerich readily conceded. But she can point to the student who learned to tamp down anger instead of fighting or the isolated student who pushed herself to join school activities. "When a student doesn't give up, we consider that success too. Maybe in other communities, that's not enough. Here, it's a lot."

Simply listening to students is one of the most powerful actions they can take, adults at Fenger agree. "At this school, they go all out around the student's emotions. They ask, they listen," said Taylor. "Me, I feel comfortable here. I don't wake up and think, 'Oh, I hope this don't happen. I hope that don't happen.' You go in with an open mind and a clear mind and you think like, 'I'm okay. I'm fine. I'm ready to learn.'"

Coaching Behavior Skills

The halls of Fenger are lined with posters that spell out the how-tos of social skills: how to ask permission, disagree appropriately, work with others, get the teacher's attention, accept criticism, and more. They come from the Kansas-based Boys Town and its manual, *Teaching Social Skills to Youth*, which features step-by-step behavior components of 182 social skills from the basic (following instructions) to the complex (resolving conflict).

"You can't hold kids accountable for something you've never told them," Erin Green, Director of National Training at Boys Town, said. "Behavior should be treated like academics, and students should be taught the skills they need to execute desired behaviors."[11]

In the summer of 2010, the entire Fenger staff traveled to Boys Town in Omaha for intensive training. They learned how to break into small, manageable parts essential social skills such as how to make an apology. They recognized that something seemingly as simple as following directions is not simple for someone who has never learned to do it. They practiced changing their own ways of responding to student behavior, both appropriate and inappropriate. In future they would set expectations and then catch students being good; when a student needed correction, they would teach a replacement behavior.

MAKING AN APOLOGY

- Look at the person.
- Use a serious, sincere voice.
- Say "I'm sorry for" or "I want to apologize for."
- Explain how you plan to do better in the future.
- Say "Thanks for listening."

The sum, staff believed, would add up to something greater than the parts: a new spirit, a new code of ethics, to replace the negative climate that made Fenger a place nobody wanted to be. Robert Spicer, whom Dozier had hired as chief dean and who had forged the link to Boys Town, acquired a new title: Culture and Climate Coordinator. And since all Fenger staff members had received training (as did new hires in successive years), consistency became the norm. Teachers and administrators shared the same expectations, techniques, methods, and language to teach and talk to their students.

The investment quickly began to pay off. "Any student who has been here for six months," said Alondra, a member of Fenger's peer jury, "will know the 'right' way to make an apology or how to disagree appropriately."

Ebony Grisby-Terry, one of the few pre-turnaround teachers rehired by Dozier, talked about a rise in "solutionary" behavior. When Darius, a ninth grader, spoke in advisory of his confusion in history class, she turned to the group: "How do you ask a teacher for help when you're confused and don't understand?" After several suggestions, students agreed on the best approach: asking the teacher after class for an appointment to talk. "Tell the teacher you want to do well in their class, but that you're confused," one student advised, and the teacher cheered. "That's what you call solutionary behavior," she declared.

Peace Circles and Peer Juries

When Robert Spicer joined Fenger in 2010, he had already developed an abiding interest in the practice of restorative justice. For six years he had worked with Chicago's Community Justice for Youth Institute, managing a program that resolved youth crime and conflict through community panels instead of juvenile court.

He had also become part of a movement among community-based organizations in the city to provide alternatives to zero tolerance policies, which a growing body of research has blamed for pushing more black and brown students toward jail than toward college.

At Fenger, Elizabeth Dozier invited Spicer to build a program that put creative conflict resolution at the heart of the school's culture. "She gave me the license to design and craft, to make mistakes and evolve," Spicer explained. "There's no cookie cutter to this. I believed that if we built something powerful, the students would come."

Spicer turned to the indigenous ritual of peace circles, a structured process for discussion and problem solving that allows every voice to be heard with respect and attention. Participants sit around a centerpiece (often a candle) and are handed a talking piece (an object with meaning to the group) when they want to speak. "At first the students were like, 'What is this kooky stuff you're doing? Voodoo? Lighting a candle? Naw, I ain't trying that!'" Within a month, according to Spicer, students were asking for peace circles all the time—with their teachers, their friends, their enemies, their parents.

"We've had twenty people fill a circle in this room," Spicer said. "It's become a sacred space, where young people can speak, share, and be heard. They learn how to disagree with someone and still be their friend."

Peer jury—the mediation that soothed Brianna at the start of this chapter—provided another antidote. Unlike peace circles, which bring together all parties in a conflict and aim for understanding, peer juries tap two or three classmates, trained in mediation, to handle a specific infraction. The peer jurors, along with an adult supervisor, meet with the student offender and together create a contract for righting the wrong. "Every issue is different, and just like a doctor, when the patient comes in, you ask them, 'What's hurting you?'" Spicer said. "In my case, it's the emotional area. I ask a series of questions, and then I determine whether it's a peace circle or a peer jury or a family conference." Whatever the decision, participation is voluntary.

At Fenger, as in schools nationwide that have embraced peer juries as a tool in restorative justice, a student who has broken a school rule sits in a circle with trained student jurors.

"We try to repair the harm that was done," explained Jason, one of a dozen peer jurors in 2013. "It may be something huge, it may be something small. We ask about the harm that was committed and how we can fix it. We try to find common ground, to help the student get back on track and act peacefully towards the person they harmed."

Alondra, another peer juror, took it a step further, explaining that peer jury also involves building the community "that's supposed to be." It's about "building trust among students and with teachers, about helping the teachers understand us—and our understanding ourselves—and then having a relationship that helps both of us," she said.

As peers, of course, Jason and Alondra walk in their classmates' shoes. Since they are going through the same things that their peers are going through, trust flows more naturally.

Students often approach them in the hall with a question or a concern. "It's part of our job, it's like we're peace ambassadors," said Alondra. "If something is amiss in the school, if something isn't going right, then we should be the ones to be able to fix it . . . maybe not fix it, but help make the situation better."

Fenger's federal grant allowed the school to make peace building a full-time priority, and Principal Dozier set a clear expectation that at least 40 percent of each week's infractions would be handled by a restorative practice. People always asked Spicer, he noted ironically, how the school set aside time for so much peace building. Were kids pulled out of class? Did it happen mostly at lunch or after school? "It happens whenever it needs to happen," he always replied.

"It doesn't make sense to say, 'Okay, well, we can only do it at this time and only for this amount of time,'" Spicer continued. "What's important is to make sure the young people understand that we'll take whatever time we need to ensure that they get what they need to move forward."

Empowering Teacher–Student Relationships

Many Fenger teachers said that knowing more about their students helped them make inroads to academic learning. Students, too, said that close relationships with their teachers helped them do their best. As noted throughout this volume, both research and practice affirm the power of strong relationships to boost student engagement and persistence.

"My teachers make it known from the very first day that if we have a bad day, tomorrow's always a fresh start," said Jason. "They say, 'You're gonna be able to do this. You're gonna pass. Don't worry. I'm gonna help you.'"

Vada spoke of how her teachers went deeper: "They are a teacher, but they're also a counselor, a mentor, a mama, an uncle, however you want to put it."

As part of Fenger's turnaround strategy, the daily schedule included two formal structures that brought students and teachers together, independent of subject-matter instruction. One was a ten-minute advisory—a time for students to focus on keeping up with class assignments. The second was a thirty-five-minute class called Start, which four times weekly immersed students in lessons about self-control, academic habits, growth mind-set, and college and career readiness. Curriculum materials and on-site support from Chicago's Umoja Student Development Corporation made the program possible.

Teachers who make themselves available during the interstices of the school day, however, supply much of the grist for supportive teacher–student relationships at Fenger. "The relationships you build and the language that you use, how you talk to a student, how you communicate respect, your day-to-day interactions with kids in the hallways, after school, before school, during lunch—they all grow organically," said math teacher Dan Zummo. "It's part of the culture and climate of this school."

Such practices are voluntary, at least in theory. "We each do this in our own way, but the expectation is constant," said Zummo. During group time, he said, he would often simply sit beside a distraught student as a calming presence. His message: "I'm here, and regardless of what's going on, I believe in you."

Many of the conversations between teachers and students are restorative, moving from listening to what students have to say to talking about what they could have done differently. Assistant principal Judith Parker (who in 2014 replaced Tosha Jones, the previous assistant principal) said that CPS had asked if the school could document the frequency of these conversations. Her reply: "They happen all day."

At weekly grade-level meetings, teachers share what they know about a particular student and strategies they have found to work—or not work—in moving the student forward. "Cleveland's not doing well in my class, but he's doing well in your class," they might say. "What do you know about him? How is your relationship stronger?" They confer routinely with counselors.

Every member of the staff carries a cell phone or a two-way radio, in the case of security guards, student advocates, and administrators. "When you learn a student has lost someone in their life, you can just text it out," English teacher Ellen Lau said. "The information will get disseminated and that student will be surrounded by support: 'How can I help? How can someone else help? If it's not me, whom do you wanna talk to?'"

Building relationships with families is also part of the mix, and home visits (in the company of one of the school's student advocates) top the list of strategies. New teachers often find that extra burden daunting, said Lau, but she tells them it's essential to enlist such support. Home visits underscore that Fenger cares about the success of each student—and that the adults who live with them are part of the team.

Keeping Ninth Graders on Track

In the Chicago Public Schools, one of the most valued indicators of student well-being is whether or not they are "on track" to graduate when they leave ninth grade. First-time ninth graders are considered on track at the end of the year if they have accumulated at least five course credits and failed no more than one semester course in a core subject (English, math, social science, or science). According to a 2005 report by the Chicago Consortium on School Research, students who are designated as on track in grade nine are three and a half times more likely to graduate from high school in four years than those off track.[12] At Fenger, the on-track rate has risen sharply: from 40 percent in 2009 to 84 percent in 2014.

"There's no way your child can fail," one of Fenger's deans told the parents of new ninth graders. "If the student gives us an inch of effort, we'll give him a mile of support."

A computerized system allows teachers to enter and monitor daily student progress—homework completion, test scores, classroom participation. Every Monday, Fenger's counselors and the student advocate (reduced to one in 2014, from a high of four) receive a "failure report" listing students who fall below a passing grade of 60 in one or more classes. The reports include tenth through twelfth graders, along with grade nine.

Eleventh grader Demora, for example, had just appeared on that week's list of students falling behind. Summoned by student advocate Henry Wilborn to Fenger's attendance office, she hunched at a computer with the advocate at her side. As the quarter neared its end, Demora was showing a 56 in advanced trigonometry, and the two went through Demora's record to see what she was missing. Together they made a plan for how she would catch up and stay caught up.

The substance of the on-track reports has to do with completed assignments, test scores, and attendance. Yet both teachers and students said that the constant push to get work done serves a larger goal: helping students believe in themselves.

"Self-motivation can get you there," said Vada. "But when somebody else is believing in you, investing in you, you actually feel like, 'I have to do it!' Like it's not an option. It's a priority to do it. And the teachers here, they give us the confidence that we can do it. There's no giving up."

Wide-Ranging Professional Development

The Chicago Public Schools contract sets aside three full days for professional development each year, with schools designing their own activities. Elizabeth Dozier is quick to say that three days, scattered across the school year, falls far short of meeting the ongoing professional development needs of her staff, who must blend social-emotional and academic learning with students facing countless risks. In addition to the three districtwide professional days, Fenger teachers convene for a one-day retreat before school starts in the fall. During the year, they meet weekly for an hour in either grade-level or subject-area meetings. "And even that's not enough," said Dozier, "considering the particular challenges our teachers face and the multiple roles they play."

Nonetheless, Fenger's School Improvement Day in November 2014 provided a window into what faculty at the school care about, how they work as a team, how they negotiate school district accountability systems, and how they marshal resources to promote student success. The full day's agenda was packed with priorities for both academic and social and emotional learning (see Exhibit 5.2).

Discussions in weekly grade-level meetings center on common readings, examinations of student work, and data analysis. Teachers also routinely collaborate in informal ways. An English teacher, for example, asked math teacher Dan Zummo how he used questions to spur problem solving among his students. He volunteered not just to coach her but also to team-teach several of her classes.

As noted earlier, conducting home visits is another skill Fenger teachers must acquire. Here, student advocate Wilborn, who grew up in the neighborhood and attended Fenger in the 1970s, provides the coaching and usually accompanies teachers.

"Let the student know you're making a visit," Wilborn advises. "Wear a Fenger jacket so that when you walk onto the porch, folks don't say, 'Who are you?' When you enter the house, you have to be blind to what's going on—it could be a lot of things—unless you think there's danger. If the parent feels you're being judgmental, they'll shut down."

Experience has taught him that adults in the household will open up, once they sense the visiting teacher's acceptance. "You build rapport with them, you give them your phone number, you let them know that you are there for their child," he said. "It's a slow process, it's not jumping on a horse and saying let's go."

Becoming a Man

Young males on Chicago's South Side walk a tightrope, like their counterparts in impoverished urban neighborhoods nationwide. Rather than graduate from high school, they may be caught up in violence, arrested for crime and vandalism, or schooled in a juvenile justice setting. When Barack Obama announced the My Brother's Keeper initiative at the White House in February 2014, a Chicago high school senior who had been part of Chicago's Becoming a Man program introduced the president. "The statistics should break our hearts," Obama said. "And they should compel us to act."

Started at another Chicago high school in 2001 by the nonprofit Youth Guidance, Becoming a Man (BAM) is a dropout and violence prevention curriculum for at-risk male students in grades seven through twelve. Groups of up to twenty students meet with a trained clinician for an hour each week. Each session targets a specific social-cognitive skill, such as those described in the following sidebar.

At Fenger, one of more than forty Chicago schools hosting a Becoming a Man program, BAM is big: about a third of male tenth and eleventh graders are enrolled, and half of ninth-grade males. Participation is voluntary, and more students want to sign up than the program has spots for.

"Our male students are hungering for a program like this," said Zachary Strother, who leads the groups at Fenger. "We begin with a check-in; we sit in a circle; and everyone takes a turn telling how they are doing physically, emotionally, intellectually, and spiritually. Before long, we're asking, 'What's a man?' 'What's strength for?' 'How do we show integrity?' 'How do we respect women?'"

BECOMING A MAN (BAM) CORE VALUES

Integrity: A man is someone who is reliable, honest, in touch with his virtues, and makes amends when he loses his direction.

Accountability: A man can feel anger, sadness, or fear, but he must own his reactions to those emotions.

Self-determination: A man perseveres in reaching his goals. Self-defeating thoughts and behaviors are barriers.

Positive anger expression: A man learns coping skills and techniques to manage his anger.

Visionary goal setting: A man learns to envision his future and make clear connections between current behaviors, attitudes, values, and visions.

Respect for womanhood: A man takes a critical look at the values and actions that reflect positive experiences and appreciation for women.

Before BAM reached Fenger in 2013, Henry Wilborn had started a chapter of Man Up, a national initiative intended to help young black and Latino males most likely to fall behind or be somehow caught up in crime. That club still exists at Fenger, reinforcing social behaviors that count outside school, on the job, in the community, or as a father.

Activities like this set out to scaffold confidence and hope in youth, according to Fenger's social worker, Chris Wills. However great the threat that gangs present, he said, "A heck of a lot more kids in this neighborhood are damaged by the belief that they won't amount to anything, and that there's nothing they can do about it."

Responding Instantly

Doctors and nurses in the emergency room have a word for responding instantly: *stat.*

Circumstances at Fenger often require staff to apply the same practice. "At another school, bullying, however destructive, rarely carries the risk of turning into a schoolwide event," said Argerich, the school psychologist.

"Here, a bullying incident can quickly escalate into something even more destructive. There's no such thing as waiting until the end of the day, or the next day, to handle it." The calculus is straightforward: meeting a student's safety or physiological needs can trump everything else.

The same can be said of incidents requiring an institutional response.

On a spring day early in the CPS baseball season, Principal Dozier learned that Fenger's baseball team had forfeited yet another game. Two-way radio in hand, she immediately summoned to her office the responsible parties: security chief Keith Connor (who also oversees the baseball team); math teacher Dan Zummo, who helps coach; and Todd Dunn, the ninth-grade student advocate.

"So what's going on?" Dozier asked.

Most of the team's recruits this year, Connor told her, had one or more class failures. Under CPS policy, that keeps them out of the game until they sign an academic contract and bring up their grades. Some of the newcomers had quit after the first week, Dunn put in, and others switched to volleyball.

"So what have you been doing about it?" Dozier pressed.

The men had tried going after additional students, they said, hoping the new team hats might help. They had turned practices into study halls with the remaining athletes. They had talked with the head of baseball for the district. But the forfeitures only escalated the complications.

Dozier was adamant. "I wanna make sure I'm communicating clearly," she said. "We need a team. We need a season. We have to keep our kids occupied in the spring—they gotta have something to do. We can't just say, 'Well, they're failing,' and then that's it. You gotta pull in new boys, and you gotta push the boys. You have to get their grades up."

She pulled out sticky notes and distributed them to the group. "I want you to write down your assignments," she said. Dunn would do everything in his power to recruit more ninth graders; ditto for the tenth-grade student advocate. Zummo, the math teacher, would draw up academic contracts with all the students who were failing and closely monitor their progress. Connor would back up the others. Henry Wilborn would arrange for the physical exams students needed, including gathering the requisite parent signatures.

Less than twenty minutes after she had summoned the group, Dozier thanked the men and wrapped up the meeting. She wanted to see movement on all fronts, she made clear, when they reconvened the next afternoon. "I know it seems like an insurmountable task, but it's really not," she said. "We can do this. We can get this done."

Attendance Matters

Like all schools, Fenger wants students to participate fully in what the school has to offer. In classes, group work is the norm, and teachers mix and match students to optimize student participation. Dan Zummo, for example, uses the exit slips students turn in at the end of class, in which they jot down what they are or are not getting, to reconfigure groups; he tries to make sure that each group includes a balance of students who understand the topic at hand and those who don't.

In assemblies and over the PA system, the school takes every opportunity to publicly recognize and reward students who shine—in sports, culinary arts, performing beats, or wherever else. "We live in a community where the word *participation* is most often linked to gangs and kids make the news when they draw the cops," said former Assistant Principal Tosha Jones. "We want to change that."

The participation that matters most here is elemental: attendance. At Fenger, the sheer act of getting to school (and on time) affects student success in lasting ways and draws in staff at levels that are unimaginable in most schools.

Near the start of our visit, student advocate Henry Wilborn visited a victim of gang violence who was recovering from a gunshot wound at home to tell him, "We don't just have your back, we have your heart." Any Fenger student who is absent for three days receives a similar home visit from a student advocate or a teacher, who brings a sheaf of schoolwork along with encouraging words.

"You gotta stay the course, man," Wilborn told the student. "I want to see you in college, not a coffin. You're a smart kid, an honors student. Gang life is no life. I want to see you in school next week, you hear me. In school. I wanna be applauding you when you walk that graduation stage!"

Back in Fenger's spacious attendance office, Wilborn swept the room with his gaze. "This is the hub," he said. "School means nothing if the student doesn't show up. We help make that happen."

Research points, not surprisingly, to the correlation between attendance and school success. In "The Importance of Being in School: A Report on Absenteeism in the Nation's Schools," Johns Hopkins researchers found that chronic absenteeism (defined as missing 10 percent or more of the school year) increases achievement gaps at the elementary, middle, and high school levels. Because students reared in poverty benefit the most from being in school, the report concludes, one of the most effective strategies for providing pathways out of poverty is to get these students in school every day.[13]

Many factors lead students to miss school in communities like Fenger's. Some miss due to illness, family responsibilities, housing instability, the need to work, or involvement with the juvenile justice system. Others skip to avoid bullying, unsafe conditions, harassment, and embarrassment. Some don't attend because they, or their parents, do not see value in school or have something else they would rather do. And some stay away because nothing stops them from doing so.

Given the high stakes of attendance, Fenger staffers—all of them—do what it takes to get every student to school every day, from helping stabilize a student's home situation to handing out bus cards and winter coats. Henry Wilborn begins most mornings driving through the neighborhood, collecting kids for whom truancy is endemic. Posters throughout the school offer reminders: "Everyone starts at 100 percent." "One missed class equals a half-day absence." "90 percent is the attendance goal for the year and students will need 90 percent attendance to participate in school activities."

Twelfth grader Latoya described her own battles with attendance. "I struggled to get to school when I started Fenger," she said. "It wasn't that I disliked school or was lazy, but I'd give myself a reason why it was okay to skip, like I was too tired or no one would notice. Where I live, there's no one saying, 'You gotta go to school.' But then my English teacher told me, 'You got to be that voice.'"

Giving and Getting Respect

At Fenger, few words catalyze stronger emotions than the word *respect*. And in the Roseland neighborhood where students live, respect can be rare, both in the giving and the getting. Making respect a centerpiece of the culture at Fenger has engaged its staff and students ever since the school began its turnaround.

Respect provides a throughline, for example, in the Boys Town prescriptions for appropriate behavior. It lays a foundation in the peace circles and peer juries that animate restorative justice here. Fenger students labeled it as respect when teachers showed they cared by pushing them when they wanted to give up or remembering something they said the week before. Fenger staff pointed to examples of collegial respect: exchanges in professional development meetings or the time a colleague backed them up without hesitation.

One of the first things teachers and students do each semester is establish classroom norms. At the front of Ellen Lau's grade nine English class, a large handwritten poster spelled out the rules the students chose: "No put-downs." "Support others' ideas and thoughts." "Challenge each other to think." "Equity of voice." Signatures from every student in the class filled up the extra space.

These norms mirror the school's Academic Talk Rubric (see Exhibit 5.3), developed in 2013 by Fenger teachers and built into classroom discussions. Three of the rubric's four indicators underscored the importance of respect: the extent to which students shared out and asked for others' ideas in equal measure, behaved respectfully and created rapport with others, and built on others' ideas, seeing disagreements as an opportunity to reconsider arguments.

Engaged Learning

Corey barely picked up his pencil during his first few weeks of eleventh-grade English. "I don't want to do nothing," he told the teacher. When the class started reading Athol Fugard's book *Tsotsi*, about a young South African man growing up in apartheid, Corey lifted his head and started to listen, but he still refused to read actively. "You have to read with us!" his teacher, Ellen Lau, told him.

When the syllabus moved on to *Othello*, Lau decided to experiment with having her students act out the script in class. She and several colleagues were part of a yearlong professional development seminar, run by Chicago's Shakespeare Theater, which mentors English teachers from some of the most at-risk Chicago public schools. Guided by the theater troupe,

Lau and her colleagues had explored best practices in literacy through drama-based strategies. She decided to try those in her *Othello* unit.

Corey was among the first students to volunteer and perform for the class, and his participation seemed to have a ripple effect. "Suddenly, he was into everything," Lau recalled. "Yes, his ability level was still low. Yes, he could read, but his comprehension was poor. But he became more engaged, more willing to struggle with the reading than he was before." It was the acting, Lau believes, that helped Corey embrace the text and, in turn, awaken as a student. This is the sweet spot Fenger teachers strive to hit with all their students: engaged learning.

As noted earlier, Fenger's teachers meet weekly in both subject-area and grade-level teams. In addition, each year, they pick an instructional target for the school as a whole. The target in 2013 was authentic literacy: the intensive integration of purposeful reading, writing, and talking across the curriculum. The approach, gaining momentum nationally, had special resonance at Fenger, with the possibilities it provided for joining social-emotional learning, relevance, and the rigor of Common Core standards.

"I like the word *purposeful*," said Lau. "With authentic literacy, you are not only learning to write, but also writing to learn. Whether it's learning math or science or social studies or English, writing becomes a tool for reaching into content."

Lau and her colleagues looked for texts that would resonate with their students, perhaps offering a tool for students to reach into the content of their own lives. Reading *Othello*, students wrote in their journals about their own trials with jealousy. With *Tsotsi*, they turned to their personal experiences with stereotypes, gangs, and making decisions, bad and good. Their reading list also included Alice Walker's *The Color Purple* and Elie Wiesel's *Night*.

"They make it about us," an eleventh grader said.

Academic Press

The high expectations embedded in Common Core standards, instead of seeming daunting, dovetail with the social-emotional lessons Fenger teachers strive to impart, about perseverance, a growth mind-set, and academic behaviors. According to English teacher Amanda Long, such demanding new standards empower teachers to push hard. She tells her students that she expects great things from them. "You keep pushing and pushing, no matter how much the kids want to butt heads against you," she said. "They know you care at the end, and they want to do it for you and themselves." She recalled one student who told her she was mean but went on to thank her for pushing her so hard.

"The teachers here, they challenge your mind," said a student named Kollin. Math teacher Dan Zummo, for example, encourages his students to see themselves as problem solvers and he coaches them through the process. "I try to model it in my own actions, in how I approach the class and try something else when a lesson goes wrong," he said.

Each year, teachers at Fenger agree on a specific, cross-disciplinary academic skill they will target for the year. In 2013, as noted earlier, they chose authentic literacy and with it, academic talk: how to engage in respectful discussions that turn on evidence and not opinion. In 2014, they selected argumentative writing, a skill elevated by Common Core. In each instance, teachers received the training they needed to begin weaving the skill into daily instruction, and they created a rubric for measuring student progress.

At Fenger, one also hears a lot about differentiated instruction—providing students with multiple ways to acquire content. To an outsider, the student body at struggling schools like Fenger may seem homogeneous: poor, minority, and low performing. Inside the school, however, heterogeneity shows up everywhere. What works for one student may not work for another—one reason why the faculty's weekly subject-area and grade-level meetings hold value.

"To reach students here, teachers need to know their kids as much as their subject," said Tosha Jones, former assistant principal. "They are always evaluating, always inventing. If you do it this way, Sean will get it. If I add this, Marissa will feel challenged."

Fenger eschews tracking, visible and invisible. Honors classes are open to any student willing to put in the work, as long as student and family agree to the behavioral and academic expectations. Rather than focus on test scores—both as a gatekeeper and a goal—these classes value persistence and hard work.

Afterschool Programs and Journeys

An erasable chart just outside Principal Dozier's office provided ongoing box scores, revised weekly, on variables that Dozier and her staff watched closely: the on-track rate for all grades (not just ninth graders), overall attendance, the number of disciplinary incidents handled through restorative justice, service-learning hours, college and financial aid applications. Another metric tallied the percentage of students—typically around 75 percent—who participated that week in one or more afterschool activities. (Over half of Fenger's male students tried out for the basketball team in 2014.)

Schools that prize learning outside the classroom often turn to site placements, internships, or classroom projects that take students into the community. These opportunities are scarce at Fenger—by default and not design. The blight and violence in the surrounding Roseland neighborhood vitiate community-based learning, and inadequate public transportation makes leaving the neighborhood equally problematic.

Not surprisingly, Dozier spent a portion of Fenger's 2010 federal grant on a raft of new afterschool activities: a mentoring program, drum line, dance, cooking, multimedia, spoken word, leadership, visual arts, a citywide student voice initiative called the Mikva Challenge, and much more. As Dozier said when she heard that the school's baseball team had yet to play a game, "They gotta have something to do." Social worker Wills talked of normalcy: "We want our kids to have the same opportunities the kids in suburban Naperville have—to play, not just to learn, but to play and feel safe."

As hoped, the new afterschool programs offered occasions for personal growth.

Daniesha described the sense of importance she felt as she and other members of her culinary arts team competed in a citywide "healthy school lunch" challenge. Aris talked about finding his voice through the Mikva Challenge and speaking up at a public hearing on zero tolerance policies.

Meanwhile, several new donations underwrote special trips to local events, college campuses, and destinations as far away as New York City. Many Fenger students had barely left their Roseland neighborhood; these trips gave them the chance to see a world-class dance company, a university classroom, the art installations in downtown Chicago's Millennium Park, the view from the Empire State Building. Like the afterschool programs, they provided an opportunity for youth to actually imagine themselves in a world outside Roseland.

The Embarc program, started by a group of Chicago teachers who wanted to stretch their students' cultural boundaries and aspirations, offered thirty Fenger students another opportunity to spread their wings. Every month, they joined Embarc students from three other city high schools on a "journey"—for example, to the teen technology center YOU-media, where they could learn to shoot and edit film, or to Chicago Ideas week, an annual gathering of world thought leaders. Once a week, they met and reflected on their journeys, practiced team-building and other social skills, or listened to an inspirational speaker.

"I learned that the world doesn't end at West 111th and Halsted," one senior said. "I've seen what's out there and I got a map."

"I Matter and I Can"

When Fenger seniors Vada and Abryanna and 128 classmates collected their diplomas in June 2013, they were part of Fenger's 100th graduating class—and the largest since Derrion Albert's killing in September 2009. They had been ninth graders when his death drew international attention to their school.

The two young women were also among the roughly sixty-five students headed to college in the fall, a 12 percent increase from the previous year.

"It feels fantastic," Vada told a reporter from the *Chicago Tribune*, making victory signs with her hands. When she entered Fenger in ninth grade—one of the few students to transfer into the school rather than out after Albert's death—her grades ranked her number 288 in a class of roughly 350. When she crossed the graduation stage this hot June night, Vada ranked fifth in her class (of 130) and was headed to study accounting at Illinois College.

"I've had a lot of proud moments at Fenger," said Abryanna, but the three full and one half-tuition scholarships she received topped her list. "When I received 'em, it was just like, 'Wow! Really? Me?' I did better than I thought I could and than I thought I did."

What motivated the students who collected their diplomas at Fenger High School's 100th graduation ceremony, in a larger community where dropping out was the norm? For some students, a drive to prove doubters wrong fueled their push to succeed. "I ain't going to be a statistic, a number in the dropout column," Latisha told the *Chicago Tribune*. "Not me." A dream, perhaps to be the first in the family to go to college, sustained others: "I want to show my younger brother and sisters what's possible." "I want to make my mama proud."

All the students agreed, however, that what kept them going most was the support system that surrounded them at Fenger. Peace circles. One-on-ones. Counselors ready to soften trauma and anger and teachers ready to listen. A culture of respect. A curriculum that welcomed students' personal experiences and stories. Teachers who never gave up, who helped students believe in themselves. Marcus, who never thought he would graduate from high school, summed it up, "Fenger taught me that I matter and I can."

RESULTS AND SUSTAINABILITY

In 2010 when the Obama administration announced its intention to use $5 billion to "turn around" the nation's five thousand poorest-performing schools in five years, it was a bold challenge. The education sector had achieved some success turning around individual schools but had little experience working at scale. The term *turnaround* had been borrowed from the business world, where low rates of success were the expected norm. Advocates and skeptics alike worried openly about how to track progress clearly and how to know when a school had actually turned around.[14]

These ambiguities notwithstanding, by 2014 Fenger had become a poster child for how a deeply troubled school could turn around—just as it had been a poster child for school violence after the Derrion Albert beating.

Despite a relentless tide of violence across Chicago's most troubled neighborhoods, including Roseland, the number of serious misconduct cases at Fenger fell from 850 in 2010 to just over 120 in 2014. Fewer than a dozen students were arrested—a fraction of the 300 arrests in the 2009–2010 school year. During the same period, the dropout rate fell from 20 percent to 4 percent. Attendance rose 11 percent. The percentage of ninth graders on track for graduation more than doubled, and the graduation rate increased by a quarter. Postsecondary enrollment grew 19 percent. In June 2013, Fenger was one of six high schools across the city that had improved most on the indicators CPS tied to college success, including course performance, attendance, academic skills, and good behavior.

Test scores remained problematic—although raising test scores had never been an overriding goal at Fenger, where teachers may spend more time helping students engage in academic talk than in test prep. While the percentage of Fenger students meeting or exceeding state standards had doubled in three years, it was still less than a third of the districtwide average of 54 percent. Only 4 percent of Fenger students achieved a combined score of at least 21 on the ACT (up 1 percent from 2010) classifying them as "ready for college coursework," compared to 27 percent citywide. At the November 2014 School Improvement Day described earlier, Fenger staff was asked to gather by the metric to which they felt most accountable. Only three of twenty-nine teachers chose test scores; the rest chose on-track status and attendance.

On the other hand, more Fenger students were headed to college in 2013 than had been the case for years. Like Vada, some had won scholarships they never thought would be theirs.

Managing Loss

As Principal Dozier and her staff faced the end of their three-year school improvement grant—and the web of social and emotional supports the grant had made possible—they continued to hope that these accomplishments would translate into ongoing funding from other sources. But that did not happen.

When Fenger opened in September 2013, therefore, it had lost more than a quarter of its staff, including ten teachers, two counselors, a dean, the full-time psychologist, and four security guards (who at Fenger played an important role in de-escalating conflicts). Afterschool programs and field trips also took a hit, although two programs (Mikva Challenge's citywide student voice program and Embarc, with its local journeys) agreed to waive the participation fee they normally charged schools.

With the start of the 2014–2015 school year, managing loss had risen to the top of Principal Dozier's job description. Over the summer, she had to dismiss the four student advocates, although Henry Wilborn agreed to stay on at half the pay (technically as a security guard). She had to let two more counselors go. Robert Spicer decided to move on and his position ended. The contract with the Umoja Student Development Corporation ended, shutting down the Start class where students had worked on interpersonal skills for thirty-five minutes every morning.

Dozier kept returning to the premise that had defined the school's turnaround strategy at the start: the social and emotional health of students would serve as a stabilizing force in students' academic growth. One month into the new school year, she exchanged two teachers and a dean for two additional counselors with mental health training. Worried that the low reading levels of incoming ninth graders would augur their early failure, she doubled their class time for reading and shifted staff to cover the increase.

With great reluctance, Dozier asked staff members who already wore multiple hats to put on even more. "Everyone was doing more with less," Dan Zummo said.

The principal also took on a new challenge: to prevent the newly college-bound Fenger graduates from succumbing to "summer melt." Nationally, some 20 percent of college-enrolled high school graduates do not show up on campus in the fall, and among minorities and first-generation college students, that rate increases to almost 40 percent. Submitting deposits, negotiating financial aid agreements, verifying FAFSA and securing loans, arranging for housing, and more can be too complicated for these students to confront, more so when they lack the financial resources to even enroll.[15]

Fenger's outsize success in college-going graduates from 2013 had attracted public attention in the CNN series *Chicagoland*, so Dozier turned to crowdsourcing for help, raising $100,000 to meet their expenses and needs. Fenger's college counselor, Blondyne Browning, began meeting with those students right after graduation. She spent the summer ferrying kids to college campuses around Chicago and across the state, showing them the ropes, paying the fees they couldn't afford, and helping them hold on to the belief that they were college material. "I needed to get in there fast," she said, "before the self-doubt grew."

Fenger teachers also set their own challenge: restoring some variation of the advisory and Start programs that had disappeared when turnaround funds ended. Ellen Lau and her colleagues planned to wrest twenty-five minutes daily from the forty-minute lunch hour for what they called micro-advisories.

Looking Ahead

Principal Dozier once quipped that she had used her turnaround funds to "buy parents for my kids." In a community where parenting is in short supply (and having a father in and out of jail is the norm), Dozier had it right. The social and emotional triage her students need is unremitting, as long as poverty ravages their families and their neighborhood. Effective structures and practices—which Fenger largely put in place—require people to bring them to life and root them in the organizational culture. At Fenger, that means *extra* people, particularly people experienced in intervening in the lives of adolescents scarred by trauma.

"Of course we want to promote resiliency in our students, to teach them to advocate for themselves," said Dozier. "But we also need to guide them every step of the way. They need a human web underneath them to get from point A to point B. Without that, they will just fail. Kids who have all the potential in the world will simply fail." Funding formulas are pegged to student enrollments, and Dozier knows that CPS is making those formulas stricter than ever. Still, she argued, "Each of our kids should count for three."

Her implication is clear: It takes *extra* dollars to address the social-emotional harm and academic deficits that Fenger students carry with them to school. Without this investment—restorative in every sense—Fenger (and schools like it nationwide) will never be able to do all they can to help their students build successful lives. Those who know the steep costs of incarceration and unemployment, endemic in the "south sides" of so many American cities, have long argued that the additional funds invested in these youth, while still in school, are an enormous bargain. "Why can't we get this?" Dozier asked.

Long-held policies concerning school size also cloud Fenger's future. The four other schools in this volume are small by design. They reflect decades of research confirming that small schools, with the structures, practices, and values their size makes possible, serve students well—often much better than the "comprehensive" high schools they seek to replace.

As of this writing, enrollment at Fenger High (once in the thousands, now approximately 350) made it the smallest of the five schools profiled in this book (on a par with Quest Early College High School). Fenger's political context, however, makes small enrollment a liability and not an asset, marking it as a failing school. Indeed, it may spell the end of Fenger in a school system that routinely closes schools when they become "too small."

"What if three hundred to four hundred students is the optimum number for a school that serves students with such overwhelming needs?" asked Chris Wills, who became Fenger's new social worker after CPS closed the Chicago high school where he used to work. "What if our small size is one of our biggest assets and not a liability?"

Before signing on as Fenger's new assistant principal in 2014, Judith Parker had worked at three other turnaround schools. Fenger's biggest asset, she remarked, might be invisible if one weren't looking for it: the social-emotional learning that courses through every interaction.

"You see it everywhere," she said. "Greeting students at the door, resolving conflicts within the classroom, teachers pulling kids aside and asking how they're doing, counselors and teachers conferring about how to help a student, teachers challenging students, then giving them the supports they need to succeed, a climate where respect flows both ways."

Parker paused, then added: "This is a school where no one gives up."

EXHIBIT 5.1   STRENGTHS AND DIFFICULTIES QUESTIONNAIRE

For each item, please mark the box for Not True, Somewhat True or Certainly True. It would help us if you answered all items as best you can even if you are not absolutely certain. Please give your answers on the basis of this student's behavior over the last six months or this school year.

Student's name _____ Male/Female

Date of birth _____

	Not True	Somewhat True	Certainly True
Considerate of other people's feelings	☐	☐	☐
Restless, overactive, cannot stay still for long	☐	☐	☐
Often complains of headaches, stomach-aches or sickness	☐	☐	☐
Shares readily with other youth, e.g., pencils, books, food	☐	☐	☐
Often loses temper	☐	☐	☐
Would rather be alone than with other youth	☐	☐	☐
Generally well behaved, usually does what adults request	☐	☐	☐
Many worries or often seems worried	☐	☐	☐
Helpful if someone is hurt, upset or feeling ill	☐	☐	☐
Constantly fidgeting or squirming	☐	☐	☐
Has at least one good friend	☐	☐	☐
Often fights with other youth or bullies them	☐	☐	☐
Often unhappy, depressed or tearful	☐	☐	☐
Generally liked by other youth	☐	☐	☐
Easily distracted, concentration wanders	☐	☐	☐

EXHIBIT 5.1   *(continued)*

Nervous in new situations, easily loses confidence	☐	☐	☐
Kind to younger children	☐	☐	☐
Often lies or cheats	☐	☐	☐
Thinks things through before acting	☐	☐	☐
Steals from home, school or elsewhere	☐	☐	☐
Gets along better with adults than other with other youth	☐	☐	☐
Many fears, easily scared	☐	☐	☐
Good attention span, sees work through to the end	☐	☐	☐

Courtesy of Fenger High School

EXHIBIT 5.2   FENGER SCHOOL IMPROVEMENT DAY AGENDA

Time	We will	In order to	Owner	Deliverable(s)
8:00–8:15	Analyze the barriers and the supports for our work this year	Build community and encourage one another	Sgts. G. & L.	A wall of encouragement
8:15–8:40	Review the new CPS Student Quality Review Policy (SQRP) for measuring annual school performance	How will our work this year tell the story of our school? What do we need to do as a team to impact student achievement? What commitments do we need to make to ensure that we deliver best practice to students?	Assistant principal	A school-wide commitment to do three things well
8:40–9:05	Review two calendaring protocols for multiple assessments of student progress: ThinkCERCA and Mastery Connect	Create a plan for monitoring and analyzing student progress over the second quarter	Teachers (S. and L.)	Calendar of assessments and commitments; staff's needs for further learning
9:10–10:00	Learn how to use encouragement to push rigorous thinking and engagement	Leverage social-emotional strategies and build resilience with our students as they grapple with more challenging tasks	Teacher (Z.)	A strategic plan to promote "productive" struggling

Time	Activity		Owner	Outcome
10:10–11:10	Breakout: Problem solving in reading and science	Use two reading strategies—close and reciprocal reading—to support students in reading complex texts in social science, science, and electives	Teachers (B., L., M., K., and R.)	Action plan for including more time for students to read complex texts in the second quarter
11:10–12:10	Develop a rubric for argument/academic writing	Identify and refine school-wide criteria for assessing argument/academic writing	Teacher (L.) and assistant principal	A framework for argument/academic writing that can be applied across disciplines
12:10–1:00	Lunch			
1:00–1:10	Energizer			
1:10–2:10	Review and update our CPS data-driven instruction calendar	Determine next steps after the data is returned to us		Compliance with CPS corrective instruction plans and data analysis protocols
2:10–2:15	Debrief the day	Identify strengths of our meetings and ways to make our collaboration better	Assistant principal	Feedback that will make us a stronger team and better able to implement SEL and academic learning in a seamless way
2:15–2:20	Launch	Gain inspiration for the work ahead of us	Assistant principal	

Courtesy of Fenger High School

EXHIBIT 5.3   ACADEMIC TALK RUBRIC

	4	3	2	1
Contribution to group (equality of voice)	Student shares out 3+ times and asks for others' ideas.	Student shares out 3 or fewer times and encourages.	Student shares out 1–2 times and/or hogs airtime.	Student does not participate and/or prevents people from speaking.
Respect and rapport	Student is respectful, uses appropriate tone, pays attention, and keeps others on task.	Student is respectful, uses appropriate tone, and pays attention.	Student is respectful and uses appropriate tone.	Student uses negative, disrespectful language with sarcasm and/or putdowns.
Citing textual-quantitative evidence	Directly quotes text AND uses ideas from text to support claims. All responses connect to textual-quantitative evidence.	Directly quotes OR uses ideas from text to support claims. Most responses connect to textual-quantitative evidence.	Uses ideas from text, but ideas may not be connected to claims. A few responses connect to textual-quantitative evidence.	Doesn't use textual-quantitative evidence throughout entire discussion. If evidence is used, it is used incorrectly.

Quality of contribution	Builds on others' ideas by agreeing or disagreeing with reasoning or with additional/new evidence. Pushes discussion by questioning or responding in a way that pushes everyone to reconsider arguments.	Builds on others' ideas by agreeing or disagreeing with reasoning or with additional/new evidence. Pushes discussion by responding in a way that pushes everyone to reconsider arguments.	Builds on others' ideas by agreeing or disagreeing with reasoning or with additional evidence some of the time.	Instead of building on others' ideas, only puts own arguments into the discussion without consideration of where the discussion is already moving.

Courtesy of Fenger High School

"A Big New Life"

Oakland International High School
Oakland, California

IDEA AND CONTEXT

If you are a new student at Oakland International High School, there comes a point—after the district has tested your English proficiency, after your intake interview, after your long journey by city bus to the low-slung school building in the Temescal neighborhood—when you will find yourself alone and afraid in the Tower of Babel.

Maybe, like Elen, you can catch at least some of what people are saying. After fleeing Eritrea through Sudan, she spent six months in a displaced persons camp in Texas, where she picked up some Spanish but little English. Now she lives in Oakland with an older sister, working at Burger King to help with her keep. Her father died four years ago; for six years she has not seen or spoken with her mother in Eritrea, though she keeps hoping to find her somehow. When she started ninth grade at Oakland International four years ago, the weight of all she carried kept her silent. "Some people, they just get shy and they don't want to talk to other people," Elen said, remembering that anxious time. "I know how it feels . . . maybe they won't like me."

Other students express their fears more actively. In El Salvador, Pedro learned to steel himself against gangs, and when he started school in Oakland, he kept his guard up. At first, "I get in a lot of trouble," he recalled. "I don't listen to the teachers, I do whatever I want. All my days I passed in the office."

In this city known for its crime rate, finding one's place outside school matters equally. "Our students get jumped a lot," said Lauren Markham, who manages family and community programs for the school. "Newcomers are often targets: robbed at gunpoint, beat up or threatened, their backpacks stolen." As Elen noted softly, "Some people, they see you on the bus, they don't look at us like people. They know us as immigrants, but they don't know we work hard."

A School for Newcomers

The student-made banners above the walkway into Oakland International High School lend a ceremonial air of welcome to this school for new immigrants to the United States. Fluttering in a light breeze, their words and symbols evoke the lives, hopes, and beliefs of the youth who painted them: "We are immigrants." "We dream of a United States without racism." "We are a community."

Since its 2007 founding, in both design and daily life Oakland International has forged that sense of community with its students, who come from thirty-three countries and speak at least that many languages. As part of the Internationals Network for Public Schools (conceived in New York City in 1985 and now numbering seventeen schools and academies in three states), the school brings very heterogeneous groups of learners into project-based academic, arts, and technology classrooms, integrating English language development in all content areas.

Fully a third of the almost four hundred students here are refugees from war-torn countries, and at least 25 percent come with little or no formal education. The district allows them to choose Oakland International if they are under eighteen, have recently arrived in the United States, and score below a certain level on the state's English language development test. Once enrolled, they may stay on as long as they are working productively toward graduation; youth of very different ages as well as languages work side by side in each grade level. The exigencies of immigrant life make its population especially transient. In any given year, 15 to 20 percent of the school's students relocate; but if they return, it will welcome them back.

The social and emotional aspects of learning have particular salience in this context. Almost all students suffer from the trauma of dislocation, the burden of poverty, uncertainties about immigration status, and an inability to communicate across multiple language barriers. Many have crossed the border into the United States without papers or parents; in spring 2014 alone, more than forty unaccompanied minors enrolled at Oakland International. The city of Oakland has its own dangers, including gang rivalries and gun violence; simply getting to and from school on city transit presents a lengthy ordeal to most students here. Yet the school is considered exceptionally successful with these students, in large part because of the way it prioritizes social and emotional factors.

Integrating Personal Histories

Entering students join a mixed cohort of one hundred ninth and tenth graders with extreme variations in their ages, English proficiency, cultural norms, and prior education. As they encounter the unfamiliar norms of the school—from cooperative learning to conflict resolution—problems inevitably come up among them. "We're really teaching kids to do school in a different way," said the school's founding principal, Carmelita Reyes, who recently received the district's Educational Leadership Award and who shares her position with a coprincipal, Sailaja Suresh.

Oakland International is organized on the understanding that such factors profoundly affect the ability to learn. When tensions arise, adults and students here use "talking circles" to restore understanding among those involved. Members of a talking circle agree on norms and typically pass around a chosen object called a "talking piece" to promote equity of voice and respectful attention. Students practice the technique in their advisory groups, which meet four days a week in forty-minute sessions; staff members also use it, to think through difficult issues. Students regularly access mental health services in many languages on school premises, provided by partnerships in the district's trailblazing Full Service Community Schools initiative.[1]

Within that framework of support for both academic and social-emotional development, Oakland International nurtures in its adolescent learners the vital understanding that their family stories of struggle can inform a larger autobiographical narrative of resilience and possibility. With the entire staff behind them in a school climate marked by extraordinary empathy, students here learn to integrate their personal histories into the experience of acquiring core knowledge and skills, increasing their fluency in English, and navigating new cultural challenges. This chapter focuses on how four major entry points—soccer, technology, visual arts, and collaborative academic discourse—engage these young immigrants in that life-changing process.

THE SCHOOL IN ACTION

Adapting to a new environment, culture, and language inevitably brings up feelings of isolation and confusion, and in adolescence these can pose even greater challenges. "There's a lot of misunderstanding," said Thi Bui, a founding teacher here and herself an immigrant in childhood from Vietnam. "If someone else is speaking in another language and looking vaguely in their direction, students think they must be saying something bad about them." That sometimes leads to fights, she noted, especially among boys in their early teens who are trying to establish their place in the school.

In order for these newcomers to fulfill their rich potential, transforming such painful frustration through language proficiency has become the work of every educator in this school. Throughout the academic curriculum and in afterschool activities, social and emotional elements undergird every step of that process.[2]

From Empathy, Language Emerges

The classroom environments and routines at Oakland International intentionally immerse students in warm support for their language development. Students typically work together at tables of four or five, carefully assigned so that a more fluent same-language peer can encourage and translate for a newcomer. Smartphones and computers are readily at hand, providing instant translation as needed. Instructions on the walls pair simple and clear language with pictures. (One poster offered tips for helping others as they speak in English: "Stay positive! Speak clearly and slowly. Listen to what they say. Repeat the same idea using different words. Act out what you mean.")

"Even the people who spoke Spanish didn't understand what I was saying," recalled Zelia, who was one of the school's youngest students when she arrived from Cuba at thirteen. "We really speak differently than people from Central America." After the rigorous public schools of Cuba, she was far ahead in subjects like math but a complete novice on the Internet. When she and Elen met that year, the bond they formed sustained both girls through their early efforts to learn English, with Elen's rudimentary Spanish as the bridge.

Starting over with younger students can also cause frustration for older students, notes coprincipal Sailaja Suresh. Even if they are about to turn eighteen, new Oakland International students start out as ninth graders, except for rare cases who arrive with considerable formal schooling and English skills.

"It's going to take them longer now to get started on their adult lives," Suresh conceded. "But typically our students here are older, and there's probably at least one other seventeen-year-old in their group." Also, many older students feel privileged that they need not go unprepared into a daunting work environment. "They're excited to have the chance to get their bearings," said Suresh. "The government has decided that they are going to get an education. And that's a real honor for a lot of them."

Expressions of empathy and appreciation among teachers and students show up everywhere in the school. A bulletin board in one classroom overflowed with sticky notes by students giving voice to positive feelings ("I appreciate Abdul for be my brother" and "Thank you Wadhah for helping me in this class"). When a misunderstanding does erupt, the assumption is always that communication will resolve it. Translators assist at mediated conversations in the school offices; if something more serious seems amiss, a student can visit a counselor privately. Vilma Ortiz, who staffs the school's front desk, knows every student personally and provides motherly direction no matter what problem presents itself.

Each student also has one teacher who serves as an adviser, ready to help and troubleshoot as needed. Amina, a student from Yemen, transferred to Oakland International after a miserable three weeks at a large high school nearby. "When the teacher asked me anything in class, I just cry," she remembered, but a reassuring hug from her adviser dried her tears and kept her going. "They will help you if you want the help."

Along with a common language, students said, their trust and friendships developed over time. "Everybody always asks each other how to say the bad words in their language," Thi Bui noted wryly, adding: "And also how to say 'I love you.'" Those who once depended on the empathy of peers began to reach out to others in their turn.

"Once I saw one of my classmates on the bus get in a fight," recalled a girl named Kamilah, from Liberia. "He really didn't understand what was going on when this boy started fighting him." As she watched in dismay, another classmate with better English stepped in to mediate. "When I saw him the next day, I said 'Thank you for helping him'—it was unfair that that happened to him."

Elen, now eighteen, volunteers at a nearby public library as part of the internship class most students take in the upper grades. Her English has reached the same level as her Spanish, she said. She aspires to study nursing at a nearby college and then move to Minnesota, where she once visited a friend of her family. "It was fresh," she said. "And I just want to have a new life." Equipped to beat the odds—in Eritrea, girls often leave school to marry after ninth grade—once more Elen is setting out to start over.

Soccer as Unifier

If asked to name one object that they recognized with relief and pleasure as soon as they started at their new school, most students at Oakland International would probably point to a soccer ball. As the world's most popular sport—played in over two hundred countries by anyone with access to a ball, a patch of land, and a few sticks for goalposts—soccer has cross-cultural appeal. At this school, it also provides an ideal way for students to forge social and emotional bonds even without a common language.

Early in the school's history, a partnership with the nonprofit Soccer Without Borders sprang from the teaching of soccer in physical education class. Led by Ben Gucciardi, it grew like wildfire; roughly a third of all students here now take part, playing on various teams that compete in Oakland and its surrounds. However, the program goes far beyond athletic competition. It encompasses youth development and leadership as well as academic monitoring, intervention, and support. "My soccer program, they always support me, everywhere," said Régis, a student from Democratic Republic of the Congo. "My personal life, on the field, academically— they're always there for me."

"Honestly, it's the cheapest therapy that we have found," said coprincipal Carmelita Reyes. "Kids can belong and be themselves and be successful starting on day one. You don't have to be good; the program takes all comers. We play fall, winter, spring, and then they get together over the summer. It's a continuous community and a continuous mentoring relationship with the coaches."

First priority, Coach Gucciardi emphasized, goes to establishing an open-door culture of inclusion and acceptance. "Regardless of language, culture, ethnic identity, gender, sexual orientation, skill level, whatever—in this space everybody can get out there and just be themselves, and get encouragement and positive reinforcement," he said. "It's okay to be competitive," he added, cheerfully acknowledging the rivalries of older adolescent boys in particular.

Unlike the boys who take part in the program, for cultural reasons almost none of the girls at Oakland International have played soccer before. Bilen, an older student from Eritrea who had recently enrolled at the school, stepped onto the field in boots one afternoon at the invitation of some other girls. Before long, she was happily lacing on some athletic shoes from the storage locker and encouraging a younger girl from her country to join the fun despite her father's disapproval. ("It's just exercises," others coaxed, to no avail.)

Simply to enjoy "silly, goofy, physical fun" out on the playing field, noted Gucciardi, "is such a leap in terms of societal gender roles" for many young women. Katie Nagy, one of two female coaches for the program's girls teams, agreed. "It takes some convincing," she said. "We talk to their families and provide a different perspective on what the sport can do for their daughters in life."

Building Bonds Across Boundaries

By bringing together peers who may not otherwise meet in academic classes, students made clear, the soccer program expands their social network. "If we see each other outside practice, we say hi to each other and ask about how the classes are going," said Feven, a girl from Eritrea. Playing together also deepens their sense of emotional safety. "We've got to know each other here," said Álvaro, from Mexico. "We don't fight. We are like a team, a family, and we feel safe."

Such cross-cultural friendships are the program's most important outcome, Gucciardi believes. For many students, he said, "the first time they build relationships outside of their language group is on the soccer field." He told of an Arabic speaker in tenth grade.

"He's really a very good soccer player whose English is still very basic. Mostly he spends time with other Arabic speakers, but through the team he's now made friendships and relationships with people from a lot of other language groups. And it's really authentic friendship, as opposed to just getting to know you. They are really invested in each other. They're teammates, and that's been a really powerful thing to see."

Many players echoed Álvaro's family metaphor in describing their attachment to the program. Hugo, who comes from Colombia, regards Gucciardi as "my second father," he said. "For him it doesn't matter the skills that you have. He is always substituting the people and make everybody play equal amount of time. No matter if we win or lose, for him what matters is that we have fun."

Régis, who captained one of the boys teams, agreed emphatically. "That's why whenever we play I give everything I have," he said. "Even though we lost, I'm still smiling. Play as hard as you can, try anything as hard as you want to try, but don't forget that we always play for fun. That's the spirit that keeps me going and loving the team that I'm in."

Their soccer coaches also serve as confidants and advisers, many students said. "If this man's going to tell you what you did wrong," said Régis, "it's like, 'I'm mad at you. Don't do this anymore. Try to change.' I like people who tell me the truth: how I did good, how I did bad, how I need to improve." He trusts his coach with personal issues, such as the need to miss practice because of child-care responsibilities at home. "He was like, 'Régis, do what you have to do, but we're here as your family too.' That was super, [to know that] there's always people there waiting for me and trying to support my life and my goals far away."

Many of her female players, Coach Nagy observed, participate less for the program's athletic or competitive aspects than for its family-like environment. "When I play soccer, it feels like a second home," said Sara, a student from Malaysia. "They feel like my real family, and we respect each other." Feven confides in her teammates or coaches when personal problems arise for her. "They're really nice," she said. "I can just talk to them about everything."

In her first year of coaching at the school, Nagy has observed the effects of the trust her players develop in each other. "Here they can come together and be part of something," she said, "with other girls they normally wouldn't associate with because of their different backgrounds." Despite their very different skill levels, "they find a common ground on the field with a soccer ball."

"Especially when you're new to this country and to this learning environment," she added, "it's hard to step outside your comfort zone and try something new. In class, you're scared to fail. But if you learn how to do that on the soccer field and then you have this support system around you, you realize that it's okay. Then it becomes okay to do that in the classroom: to learn, and to speak English, and to try all these things that are very new and very scary. Soccer creates an environment where it's safe for them to try, and hopefully it translates back."

Developing Leadership

With the young men in the program, Gucciardi sees a variation on that theme. "The male ego gets bruised when they can't speak English," he has noticed.

"And when they feel like they're bad at something, they often react with: 'I don't have to listen to you, I don't have to do this.' For those boys who are having a hard time in the other areas of their life, soccer is something that is familiar, that they're good at, that they love. They really feel invested in it, which is so important. It's something where they're excelling."

Behavior change, he remarked, takes place gradually. "It starts with some positive reinforcement when they do the right thing," he said.

"Wow, you're doing such a good job being a leader here on the field! Could you also do that in the classroom? Your English is a lot stronger than some of the other students. The same way that you're leading here, you could do that in the classroom."

The relationships among teammates and coaches reverberate in other contexts as well. In one memorable incident, a bad fight over a girl broke out between two boys from different language groups, sparking a dramatic face-off between their Arabic-speaking and Spanish-speaking supporters. At soccer practice later, the players (many of them boys from the same two language groups) decided to take a stand to calm the waters. Forty-five minutes before school started the next day, some twenty male and female teammates stood together in its entryway and greeted their peers, holding signs in many languages: "We want peace in our school."

At such moments, said Gucciardi, the Soccer Without Borders program "becomes much more than the sport itself." By stepping up to facilitate healing in that crisis, students showed the leadership and values that it stands for. "We all like soccer," the coach said. "But we're using it as a platform, a means, a vehicle for building community."

Learning Language Through (E)motion

Creating that community has had its own remarkable effect, which goes directly to the central mission of the school: helping its language learners to communicate successfully in English. "One of our rules is to do your best to speak English on the field," said Gucciardi. "And I think that really helps. There are certain times when they are just forced to speak English in order to communicate with teammates from different language groups. There's no other way."

The research on acquiring and remembering language has long linked action with words: we remember phrases like "throw me the ball" better, for example, if we are actually tossing a ball than if we study it in a textbook.[3] More recently, cognitive scientists have theorized that thought, memory, and language derive from actual motor and sensory experience. According to this view, what we know and how we reason—whether we are kicking a ball into a goal or curled up with a good book—depends on activity in the same neural systems used for perception, action, and emotion. Psychologists Arthur Glenberg and Michael Kaschak explain:

> The abstract symbols of language must be grounded, or mapped, to the world if they are to convey meaning. . . . That is, the meaning of a sentence is given by an understanding of (1) how the actions described by the sentence can be accomplished or (2) how the sentence changes the possibilities for action. . . . This description of language understanding is not metaphorical—that is, it is not simply a way to describe understanding. Instead, real bodily action is at the root of meaning conveyed by language.[4]

This understanding has important implications for how English language learners in high school enter academic discourse and come to conceptual understanding of abstract phenomena. As Glenberg and Kaschak put it, "Even as adults, we understand language about physical, social, and psychological causation in terms of the pushes and pulls of our bodily experience."

The young soccer players on the fields behind Oakland International provide a rich picture of English language proficiency progressing (quite literally) by leaps and bounds. Caught up in the physical and emotional flow of the game, they let go of their fears and call out to each other freely, reinforcing with every play their growing understanding of meaning in their new language.

"On the soccer field it was like I was in another world," said Régis. "Everything they would tell me, it would just get in my head—I was like, *ohh!*"

Feven, from the girls team, agreed with him. "It's more free outside," she explained.

"You can't say, like, 'pass the ball' or something like that in their [native] language [so] you have to use your English. You become more confident because they will still understand you—even if you don't know how to say the word, you show them with your feet. . . . You try to say those words without feeling shy or anything, because you're playing and the purpose is to score a goal. I think you develop that way. Because it's something you like to do. It's something you don't have to force."

Feven recalled watching a player strategize with her teammates at a game—first in Spanish, then switching to English. "She said she wasn't really good at speaking English, but she was going to try 'cause it was important for us to win. . . . When they're passionate about what they like, they still get up and do it because they know how soccer's supposed to be played."

"It's so awesome," said Selene, a student from Mexico. "People don't know how to speak English, so we speak our own language sometimes, and sometimes we speak English, but we can still understand each other through soccer."

Supporting Athletes as Students

Coach Gucciardi has begun exploring ways to intentionally integrate academic vocabulary—such as "evidence" and "analysis"—into the language of soccer practice. In the meantime, he and his coaching colleagues act as steadfast champions of the habits students must build in order to succeed at their coursework. Students regularly do homework at the tables that fill the Soccer Without Borders office, with help readily available.

"He's not only focused on making you a good soccer player," said Ami-lanu, who comes from Guatemala and aspires to be a lawyer. "He's also focusing on making you a successful person for the future. He don't care if you're really good at soccer. He cares if you're having a good education, you're preparing yourself for a future."

Hugo described an occasion on which Gucciardi took a group of play-ers to the home of a struggling teammate who had given up on school. "We went to talk to him, try and make him go back to finish high school, see how important it is to have a high school diploma in life," he recalled. For another player, who was strong in both soccer and academics, the coach made sure he visited university programs and met the deadlines for college entrance exams. "Who does that for you?!" Hugo exclaimed. "It's amazing. And he treats equally everybody. [He says to us,] 'Obviously you can apply too. You're going to make it.'"

Soccer Without Borders considers such support part of its core mission. Though players may struggle with academics or have issues with class-room behavior, "they are also very invested in soccer," said Gucciardi. "To help them stay focused, we can leverage their participation on the team with some academic outcomes." At such an intervention, student, family, and teachers typically confer together to agree on a plan and fair con-sequences—such as losing the right to play in games or at practices—if transgressions occur.

In other cases, students who have dropped out maintain their con-nection with learning through soccer practice. One such student, now twenty-one, left school in eleventh grade and "still comes all the time," said Gucciardi. "He's now finally decided he really wants to finish his GED, so he's coming here to get help and support." Their families trust the soc-cer coaches as well, asking assistance with everything from buying a used car to finding their way in a thicket of city agencies. Such interactions at once affirm and extend the culture of growth, opportunity, and empower-ment the program seeks to create, the coach reflected. "We're getting more intentional about that all the time."

Finding the Way Through Art

At every turn, art made by students pervades the campus of Oakland International, and—like the soccer program—visual art provides a crucial pathway toward belonging here. Student-created banners flutter over the entry walkway, declaring in bold red, white, and black the place of immigrants in the larger community. In the entrance passage hangs an array of illustrated student research and reflections on the visual patterns of textiles, currency, roofing, and other artifacts from their native countries. Most of the walls in the courtyard and corridors display huge murals that the students have painted. One illustrates with totemic figures and clasped brown hands the theme "Respect Each Other" spelled out in twelve languages; another, located near the school's garden, portrays the ecosystem in brilliant hues and bold designs; a third juxtaposes silhouettes of athletes at play against a bright green background.

Around the upper perimeter of Brooke Toczylowski's art classroom hang poster-sized black-and-white photographic portraits in which students hold up their written declarations ("I am Afghani"; "I am ambitious"). Someone has overpainted a wall poster of a red "Do Not Enter" sign with the haunting black outline of a girl's concerned face. On large round placards mounted up near the classroom clock, hand-drawn symbols illustrate the words *community, curiosity, compassion,* and *creativity.*

As Elliot Eisner suggested in his seminal book *The Arts and the Creation of Mind,* the arts teach students to attend to relationships, develop their mental and emotional flexibility, and help them use imagination to shift the direction and expression of their thinking.[5] Just so, the guiding principles of this school's art program—articulated in this classroom as "I see, I think, I wonder"—reverberate throughout the social, emotional, and academic lives of its students.

The power of art seems to play even more of a role in the development of these English language learners. Just as soccer embodies language and meaning through their physical and emotional experiences, artistic expression enlarges their capacity to create meaning as they absorb a new language and its symbol system. "I just draw and explain by doing something without speaking," said Sara. "I can't describe my drawing; it's something described for me."

"You paint something, if you don't know how to say it," added Feven. "Your painting can just explain what you're thinking and feeling. And also you get to create things that you want to say without speaking." Writing words to go with her images (as in an artist's statement) "helps you to say what you're thinking, and [what] you would say if you could speak it," she said. Pausing to think, Feven concluded, "It's like soccer. Sometimes we don't have to say anything. . . . It has its own language. We don't have to learn; we just create it."

Studio Thinking

Students created the entryway flags in a unit designed "to reimagine and reframe the conversation about immigration in the United States," said Toczylowski. She described how they began the project by studying the work of the Oakland printmaker Favianna Rodriguez, whose parents were Peruvian immigrants.

"Favianna talks about how some people compare immigrants to cockroaches invading your kitchen. But she likes to imagine immigrants as butterflies, who are able to freely move and need to migrate in order to survive, just like many immigrants. We went through all sorts of class discussions about that, and small group discussions. Working in groups, they then chose sentences that defined what they had in common as immigrants: 'We are dreamers,' or 'We work hard,' or 'We want a good education.' Then they created their own symbols for those ideas, or chose symbols that already exist. [This student's] group's flag says 'We want all people to have freedom,' and he chose the Statue of Liberty as a representative symbol of that."

The arts program here has forged close ties with Harvard University's Project Zero, whose researchers explore the processes of coming to know the world through art and thinking like an artist. With a local grant from the Abundance Foundation, teachers have joined with colleagues from nearby schools to learn how "studio thinking" in arts classrooms might extend to other domains of learning. Rooted in the concept of thinking dispositions, the approach centers on specific habits of mind and classroom structures in the teaching of visual arts.[6]

One class was exploring the word *experiment*, which many students associated with their science classes. To see what it could mean in visual terms, they were looking into the ways that artists "play." After their teacher modeled the process, they tried drawing on a magazine with oil pastels and then ripping it in half to see the resulting images. Next, they worked in their individual art journals, experimenting with collage, tempera, pastels, or different types of pen or pencil. Some students played with the surrealistic technique of "exquisite corpse," a collaborative image assembled from unrelated parts. "I see . . . it is made of lines and shapes," one student wrote, examining the result. "I think . . . it is an abstract draw. I wonder . . ."

These learners are practicing "studio thinking," but one could use much the same language in describing intellectual growth in other curriculum areas and in their daily lives. A look at the "studio habits of mind" described by Project Zero makes that apparent:

- *Developing craft* easily translates to acquiring the tools and techniques of other domains.
- *Observation* in the arts correlates to listening and attending elsewhere.
- *Envisioning* compares to generating hypotheses.
- *Reflecting, expressing, exploring,* and *engaging and persisting* all have clear relevance to any field of inquiry.
- *Understanding the world of art* correlates to understanding the larger context of any domain in which students work.[7]

In teaching the arts, the "studio thinking" approach calls for certain structures—demonstration–lectures, protocols of students at work, and critique—that also apply readily to learning in other domains. Just as Toczylowski modeled an artistic technique in her class that day, teachers in other classrooms can model the ways that historians analyze documents or scientists design an investigation. Just as their art teaching colleagues do, they can set up differentiated classroom work for students that allows observation and intervention as needed. Even the traditional critique of artwork in process offers a way for nonarts classrooms to reflect and develop understanding as a community.

Narrating Immigration Stories Through Graphic Arts

Another major art project that called on immigration stories came about in 2010, when Thi Bui, who at the time taught ninth and tenth grade art, proposed to her class that they write and illustrate their immigration stories in graphic-novel form. With a few simple conventions like panels and speech balloons, she said, students who had only rudimentary English "surprised, informed, inspired, and moved me to tears."

We Are Oakland International, the self-published book that resulted, sells on Amazon and brims with a power and pathos that belies its comic-book format. Maria's story, "My Odyssey," portrays her arduous journey with her brother from El Salvador to rejoin their mother, who had left after two earthquakes had devastated their country. On the way, as she told a public radio interviewer, "A lot of bad things happened to me. But in the end it was happy, because I met my mother after nine years."

The first two stories in the book, by a student named Bao, both appear under his title "A Big New Life" and tell of his former life in Vietnam and his family's transition to California. Bao's comic art is highly developed in both, but the story he first portrayed as a shy new tenth grader revealed little of his emotional experience. The next year, before the book went to press, Bao returned to Bui with a revised version that fairly leaps off the page with the tensions of growing up across two cultures. "Here is a young man who is becoming a storyteller," his teacher wrote in her introduction. "He is learning by figuring out what his story really is."

Technology as Agency

After seven years at the school and with experience across several curricular domains, Thi Bui was teaching technology to eleventh graders, which only increased her students' capacity to express themselves through the arts. The previous year, her class created a movie screenplay from Cory Doctorow's dystopian novel *Little Brother*, which features a diverse group of activist Bay Area teenagers. Since most of her students struggle mightily with reading, that work created a fascinating literacy experience, Bui said:

"Translating this novel's text into a screenplay format really gets them to read closely. You change everything that's past tense into the present tense, which means you have to be very aware of who's speaking every time there's dialogue. It makes you look for the action, so it actually helps you understand the text as well."

Movie making, she saw, presented a powerful learning tool. "There's always the issue at the end: your movie is better if you understood the text," she mused. "But if they can visualize the text through the movie—act it out, watch it, talk about it—then it might be more useful as part of the process of reading." So the following year, in a documentary project, she explored the uses of a storyboard activity. This time, students pieced together their footage without screenplays in a process that emphasized research skills. It was a developmental jump, she said, from the earlier graphic novel project in which they told their own stories. "In the eleventh grade, it's telling somebody else's story through your lens. It's going outside yourself."

One group began with a "literature review" of the immigration comics produced by peers in the previous year. "They identified what was still missing in the stories, what they wanted to know more about," Bui explained. "Then they created more research questions and turned them into interview questions." One team of students might interview another, often across language groups; or students might also interview a parent. A student who hails from the featured country acts as guide for the process of connecting, interviewing, and translating, but "everybody is working outside their own experience in the documentary," Bui said. "It feels nice— they're learning, and they appreciate each other."

Thinking with Computers

Like soccer and visual art, the use of digital technology across domains at Oakland International seems to infuse an ever-growing sense of agency into the learning process of these English language learners. It gives them yet another "thinking language" as they take on complex challenges across the curriculum. It provides alternate ways of expressing what they know and can do. Not least, it acts as an ever-present private "guide on the side," translating and pronouncing terms that otherwise might easily remain opaque.

The school is approaching a one-to-one ratio of computers to students and continually acquires more, with donations from the community non-profit Oakland Technology Exchange West (OTX West). Students come and go continually at banks of computers in the central area through which everyone arrives; many classrooms have a "half lab" of ten to fifteen computers for rotating use; three laptop carts make the rounds. After taking a free training class by OTX West, students and their families can take home refurbished computers and other equipment.

"It helps us a lot, learning things on a computer," said Kamilah. Every student and family has free access to language study using Rosetta Stone software. For help with translation and pronunciation, students may consult classroom computers or keep smartphones close at hand. They use computers to read books, to do research in different languages, to check their e-mail, and to share and revise their written documents. They use inexpensive video cameras that the school has bought, downloading moviemaking software that they can also access from home. On the school Web site, they can access dozens of "survival English" resources, ranging from phonics chants to vocabulary videos and easy-to-learn popular songs.

Coprincipal Sailajah Suresh, who previously taught the eleventh-grade technology class, largely focused there on developing students' technical proficiency. When Bui took it over, she thought hard about what new lens she might introduce to students. In the first year, "We talked a lot about the Internet," she said.

"The world before the Internet, what we use the Internet for now, what might it be in the future, what issues we need to think about. And this year it's a lot more focused on the students as learners. What kind of learner am I? How can technology help me learn, grow, work? And then—as they become more of a community—how do we use computers and technology to collaborate? How can you be 21st-century learners in that way? How do we use the Internet to share our work?"

One wall in her classroom displays a long timeline that students created to represent the life history of the Internet. "We always start with a blank slate," Bui said, explaining that the timeline went up during one day's lesson on evaluating the reliability of sources: "One first step is confirming your information. I had them look up when a piece of technology was invented or developed, but they couldn't put it up [on the timeline] until they got two other people to confirm a different source for the same information. It was a baby step toward being critical readers and [developing] information literacy."

Mastery in a Digital Context

In another class not long after the fall term began, Bui's students were revising essays in which they described what they would like to learn and do in the class that year. To persuade their classmates of the value of their proposals, they had also used computer software to produce short animations, selecting a background and small avatars, and then incorporating sound and movement and humor as the characters made their case.

"Mastery assignments can always be improved," read a note on the whiteboard. "You can rewrite parts of your essay or finish it for a better grade." Half the grade in this class comes from mastery of tasks like the essay or the animation, the rest on class participation, homework, and growth in English.

"I'm very, very excited because this is the first time that my students have given me so many ideas in this class," said Bui. "Not all of them want to make movies. Some are interested in taking apart a computer and understanding how it works. Some are interested in learning programming so that they can get a job." For each interest, she plans to bring in an expert they can learn from, and with each visitor they will use the same process. First "I want kids to get a window into how this person thinks," she said. Then with the expert's help, they will "take apart an object, build an object, and share that object—it could be a movie, a computer, a software program."

"Just know that it's a long year," she told her class that day. "We're going to try to do all of the things you've asked to do." They would start with a moviemaking project, she continued, joining others in a long literary and artistic tradition by creating their own "love letter to a place." Mousir, a student from Yemen who had worked on three movies the previous year, would serve as expert and set the context for his peers. In a corner of the room, he was rehearsing what he would say.

"Last year I learned that it's not easy to do a movie, so first you have to think, you have to observe around you. I would suggest they think about the thing that maybe people would like to learn about that place. Maybe they would love to see some pictures, and [I will show as an example] how an image of the Golden Gate represents San Francisco. I will teach them some steps they need . . . how to choose their song or music, the steps they need to save after the work."

"In all classes, when students think of a good idea, the teachers always support you," Mousir said in a tone of confidence and pride as he prepared to teach his peers what he had learned. "My voice counts. Teachers try to understand what students want, then do it."

Finding Oneself in the Curriculum

Identifying what matters most to adolescents takes on even more importance when teaching academic subjects to these new language learners. Their search for identity and their yearning for friendship provide an especially strong avenue to foster the knowledge and skills that will matter so much to their futures, many Oakland International teachers observed.

As a base for all their learning, Jennifer Kelly-DeWitt makes sure that her ninth- and tenth-grade English language arts students buy in to her expectation "that everyone is sharing their ideas with each other, and that those ideas are valuable." Starting the year by talking about things that already matter in their lives, she said, consolidates their understanding of that discussion norm. As examples of topics, she offered "Should you be able to have your cell phone in school?" or "Compare the merits and demerits of Oakland to those of the place you came from."

"Through that, I think kids start to feel, 'I have a place here. People are listening to me . . . I'm sharing my experience and my ideas.' Then we move from there to more text-based work, where again you have to share your ideas but it's more about a story. . . . We don't go right into reading a book. We start with something more approachable—something autobiographical or cultural."

Kelly-DeWitt's unit on ethics makes a good example of that process. Huge charts festoon her classroom walls, on which her students have written examples from the moral codes of their Buddhist, Hindu, Muslim, and Christian belief systems. (Among them: "Hating other people is a big loss to yourself." "Be peaceful." "A women cover her hair." "Don't descrimination.") Only after engaging on that personal level do they move on to discuss the moral codes of literary figures like Odysseus, the teacher said. "By being gradual, most students feel like they have at least a toehold in the work."

Belonging in the Discussion

With language skills varying so greatly in these heterogeneous classrooms, teachers here do struggle to make sure that every student engages with the target concepts. "We do have a lot of kids who *can*, to varying degrees," Kelly-DeWitt said, "and then we have kids who you could perceive as *cannot*, to varying degrees . . . in this moment." Separating them in different levels to work on the same concepts, she recalled, often ended with students "sort-of copying material they didn't necessarily understand from students who did understand."

To address that issue, she and her grade-level team have devised a discussion protocol that gives all students meaningful thinking roles in small heterogeneous groups, regardless of language proficiency:

- *Reporters* facilitate table discussion and keep it going when it falters, pressing on with another question or more examples.
- *Trackers* chart students' participation, noting as people contribute ideas, take notes, and push the conversation further.
- *Translators* interpret the group discussion in non-English speakers' home language and then ask for their comments and share them with the group.
- Everyone else has the role of *speaker*, and they may report back main ideas to the larger group.

The method takes planning. Kelly-DeWitt assigns students to a consistent group that ideally has at least three languages represented. Spanish and Arabic prevail in her classroom; usually two interpreters suffice, as many students speak yet a third language. If necessary, students can look in a dictionary or get a digital translation from a device. Though that makes the discussion less rich, she said, "it makes them feel the expectation that they're participating."

Using the protocol has markedly increased the sense of belonging among her newcomer students, Kelly-DeWitt said. They no longer feel excluded from a discussion not really about them, "because it is very clearly about them. It's changed that dynamic."

Teachers in other domains, such as history and art, found the method useful in their classes as well. Most students also said that working in small groups of students from other language groups pushed them to work hard on speaking English. "That's the way I learned," said Hugo.

Putting Emotions to Work

As students develop in their language skills and move on to eleventh and twelfth grades, teachers also provide scaffolding for the new challenges they face. For example, Thi Bui breaks down the task of essay writing into more manageable parts. She might start with a visual representation of an essay and then introduce topics that might appeal to different students. Before they begin to write, students try out thoughts with each other in brainstorming and pair-share activities, and after finishing a draft, they exchange feedback.

Writing one paragraph typically takes a day, and "each day they feel completion and some success," Bui said. By the end of a week, "they see that writing an essay"—which they must do to pass California's high school exit exam—"is not that impossible."

Ambitious content also lies well within the reach of English language learners, teachers here agree—but it too needs careful scaffolding. Working with three colleagues at San Francisco International High School, for example, Jennifer Kelly-DeWitt adapted Shakespeare's *Romeo and Juliet* for her ninth and tenth graders. The teachers knew that their students would relate to its themes of adolescent love, conflict, loyalty, and deceit; and as cultural capital the play also had high value. So they created a more accessible text that kept a "judicious amount" of the original Shakespearean language. Classes then combined close reading activities with watching Baz Luhrmann's 1996 movie *Romeo + Juliet* as well as the 1968 rendition by Franco Zeffirelli. With its many opportunities to speak, listen, read, write, and perform, the classic text seemed a good one to help students work toward Common Core ELA standards regarding such matters as textual analysis and paraphrasing.

Yet in this extremely heterogeneous class, Kelly-DeWitt's summative assessments for the unit differed. Even students with minimal English, for example, could join a small group of peers in performing an adapted scene. Many students also wrote a four-paragraph essay (one prompt: "How do characters' words and actions worsen or resolve the conflict between the two families?"). However, newcomers to the language only compared and contrasted two characters in writing and then wrote accompanying text for a complete storyboard of the play.

In adapting the play's text, Kelly-DeWitt said, she always looked for "what can stay mostly the same." She aimed to keep Shakespeare's most famous lines intact and to maintain his complex metaphors, while modifying grammar and vocabulary to help students understand. ("I had to weigh the value of each word they would not know," she said.) To mingle students of different language levels, she simplified and shortened some roles and left others longer and more difficult. Throughout the text, she inserted graphics and storyboards that gave emotional and visual cues to its meaning.

In act 1, scene 5, for instance, Romeo says that Juliet "is like a dove next to crows." Students could gather a sense of the scene from a Shakespeare edition presenting the play through comic art. They could consult a vocabulary bank of familiar words (like *ugly, beautiful, loud, annoying, peaceful, black, white,* and *pure*) to explain how Romeo viewed Juliet compared to "all the other people at the party." Or they might perform a randomly selected line from the scene, coupling it with an expressive action. Bit by bit, this teacher said, they were making the text their own—and finding themselves, at times, in the curriculum.

Seeing One's Place in History

In history classes as well, teachers draw in social and emotional elements to support students' academic understanding, and vice versa. "Whether it's a concept or a skill, we scale it down to whatever their street view is," said Veronica Montejano-Garcia, who teaches world history to ninth and tenth graders. "Then we ratchet up the demand." Prior to a unit on the Mexican-American War, she asked her class to debate the issue of students fighting each other. Once they drew their own lines about justifiable conflicts, they found more reason to engage in studying historical conflicts, she observed.

"They can see that aggression plays out in similar ways in different contexts. They begin evaluating it, defining it, describing it not just in their own lives but also in history. [They ask] 'What do I know about this?' and 'Do I think it's a problem?' and 'Do I have ideas about solutions?'"

In another unit, students analyzed what their world history textbook said about their home countries. "Many of them found nothing," she said. "So we supported them to write about how they felt about that, and what the textbook writers needed to know. They're already questioning the history book, which is great." As a culminating project for the year, students will gather and share oral histories from relatives or family friends. "I want them to be active in this class," Montejano-Garcia said. "Taking in stories, talking about stories, documenting their own stories or their families' stories."

Eleventh graders in Raquel Franker's U.S. history course begin class by responding in their journals to prompts like "Describe a time you had to change in order to fit in." Discussions also start with familiar concepts; after showing the "After the Mayflower" episode from the PBS documentary series *We Shall Remain*, the teacher asked, "If you find something that nobody is using, is it okay to take it? Is it okay to take land?"

As students learn that the United States has always been a nation of immigrants, they gain perspective on their personal obstacles. "Everything they're doing is history," Franker said. "It's not necessarily to *answer* the question: 'Where do I fit in this situation?'—more to *ask* the question and realize that there's more than one answer to that."

Unlike their peers in most U.S. schools, very few Oakland International students have studied the country's history before. To help them develop a meaningful sense of events that span four centuries, Franker builds the year around the question "What is an American?" She narrows her focus to four eras (the nation's beginning, the Civil War, the Great Depression and New Deal, and the civil rights movement), then coaches her students in taking perspectives as historians do.

From Simulation to Action

One week, for example, Franker's students were using the social networking site Edmodo to role-play characters from the colonial era. "They're either a Wampanoag or an English colonist," the teacher explained.

"And they create a historical background for that person. We want the students to understand what a primary source is, so they create their own bank of primary sources: actual images and maps. They create timelines. Then, from the perspective of their character, they communicate back and forth to each other [on Edmodo] from their different perspectives. Hopefully, by the end of the project, they'll have an idea of what it's like to be in somebody else's shoes when interpreting history, and how to do it."

In another assignment, students write two "letters home" from the perspective of their character: one before colonization and one after the colonists' arrival. Students begin to realize, Franker said, "that over time relationships change, depending on the historical circumstances around them."

After studying the role of youth in the 1960s civil rights movement, in May 2013, her class organized a whole-school teach-in about immigration reform issues that has itself gone down in history at Oakland International.

First, Franker recalled, two students spoke to the whole school: "We need to fight for this, this is important to us, this is what we're learning in history, and it's connected to our lives." Next, eleventh graders wearing armbands led ninth, tenth, and twelfth graders on a learning tour of teaching stations they had set up in the school cafeteria.

Their teacher described the stirring scene: "One station was for an e-mail writing campaign to Congress. We had instrument-making and poster-making tables. We had a letter-writing table that did handwritten letters, and we had voice recordings—and these were all about immigration and immigrant rights, just at the time when people were talking a lot about this. The cafeteria was abuzz with everybody getting excited, and then we started marching down the street."

Playing instruments and holding handmade posters, the group marched more than two miles before arriving at the downtown Oakland office of their U.S. representative in Congress, Barbara Lee. "She herself was in session," Franker said, "but students presented the letters to an aide who came down and talked to them and thanked them. It was the biggest rush we've ever had at this school."

Unified Assessment Practices

This school's emphasis on a unified approach across the faculty shows up especially in its grading practices, which spark collegial conversations across content areas every year. No matter what the academic subject, progress in English language development counts for 20 percent of a student's class grade. Showing effort in daily class work and homework makes up another part of that grade. In grades nine and ten, students can pass a class even with relatively low content mastery; but the importance of mastery increases in the upper grades.

Every spring, students present portfolios representing their year of work in all the subject areas. Teachers use a common rubric to assess those portfolios, assigning an overall grade that counts toward every class. Students upload the work in digital form, so they and others in the school community can review their progress over time.

Passing the California High School Exit Exam (CAHSEE) nonetheless may pose problems for English language learners whose skills do not advance on a sufficiently brisk schedule. In 2014, the school used grant money to launch six new classes of intensive language intervention in a "seventh period" after school. Taught by Oakland International teachers, it targets all students past grade nine whose scholastic reading inventory still ranks in the "zero lexile." It takes awhile for reading skills to catch up to spoken language skills, Reyes noted. "We want to make sure that by grade eleven, that is happening." To augment that program, in 2010 the school began the district's first summer school specifically for English language learners, serving students from any district high school as well as its own.

Oakland International has steadily grown its capacity to work with English language learners who have severe learning disabilities. It can take considerable time for immigrants to be identified as needing individual education plans, noted Ryann Pollock, who teaches the special-day inclusion class here. Most of her students participate in regular advisory groups and attend mainstream classes, with support from the school's two instructional aides. But Pollock also leads a special advisory group of five twelfth graders, supporting their reading development and working with them on the postsecondary transition. "We're trying to build social skills in here," she said, "and make it a safe place to access more knowledge."

RESULTS AND SUSTAINABILITY

That day of empowerment when students marched for immigration reform—like the Shakespeare scenes, like the soccer program, like the bold murals and the student-made films and publication—testifies to the influence that social and emotional factors exert in the intellectual development of English language learners. By placing those elements at the heart of its mission, Oakland International High School is creating a new place for young immigrants to make their own, as scholars and as people.

The high level of transiency in this school designed for immigrant youth complicates efforts to track the educational outcomes they achieve, however. For any number of reasons, many Oakland International students who enroll in grade nine cannot stay through grade twelve; others leave and then come back as their circumstances change. Of those who do remain with their cohort through senior year (average age nineteen), 55 to 60 percent typically graduate that June. After taking into account those students who stay on for a fifth or sixth year, that figure rises to 75 percent.

Coprincipal Carmelita Reyes can often only guess what happens to the remaining 25 percent who do not graduate from that typical class. She has heard that at least one of them simply enrolled in community college (through open admissions) and is now matriculating in the University of California system. But when overage students decide instead to stay on campus at Oakland International to improve their English and their readiness, she considers that a remarkable sign of trust in the school community.

Building a Unique Faculty

Hiring and developing staff members who live up to that trust, Reyes said, counts as the most important thing she does, aside from the school budget. She looks for people who have "cultural competency in other cultures—experience in being foreign and figuring things out, and who empathize with how hard that is." That awareness deepens further through an annual school tradition called the Community Walk, in which students and their parents guide teachers on an excursion through the city's immigrant communities. As they explore neighborhood resources, cultural centers, and social environments, staff members increase their understanding of the strengths and challenges their students bring with them.

Since all teachers take responsibility for scaffolding students' language development, that skill ranks at least as high as an applicant's content-area expertise; specialists in language intervention also augment the staff. Above all, Reyes looks for highly collaborative teachers, who join a team of five or six, sharing four cohorts of twenty-five students who stay together throughout the school day. Team members must work flexibly and in concert with each other, she said, "agreeing on what and how they're teaching, and how they're reinforcing it through practice." She will not even hire "superstars," she said, "if they can't let go of some things they thought were important in order to take up some group work." The team for grades nine and ten, which stays with its students for two years, has an especially critical role in providing continuity of learning and social-emotional support, she said. "It's only at the end of their first year that a teacher starts to really understand them, as students develop enough English to explain the trauma that happened wherever they came from."

Coprincipals Reyes and Suresh often accommodate teachers who wish to work part-time for family reasons, and so the teaching staff fluctuates

between twenty-one and twenty-five teachers for roughly four hundred students. Wherever possible, grants pay for additional teachers, increasing the adult-to-student ratio throughout the school. Satisfaction is high and staff attrition is rare; only two teachers left at the end of the 2013–2014 school year.

Social and Emotional Outcomes

One important way in which Oakland International tracks student success comes from the California Healthy Kids Survey, a yearly statewide survey of students that concerns resiliency, protective factors, and risk behaviors. From its reports, schools gain information on how their students perceive the school environment with respect to the following elements:

- The school has a core instructional program with qualified teachers, a challenging curriculum, and high standards and expectations for students.
- Students are motivated and engaged in learning, both in school and in community settings, during and after school.
- The basic physical, mental, and emotional health needs of young people and their families are recognized and addressed.
- There is mutual respect and effective collaboration among parents, families, and school staff.
- Community engagement, together with school efforts, promotes a school climate that is safe, supportive, respectful, and connects students to a broader learning community.

Each spring, Oakland International staff members administer the Healthy Kids survey to eleventh and twelfth graders with the necessary language skills. In the 2012–2013 school year, students gave the school high marks on the scale for its overall learning environment (as per questions pertaining to caring relationships, high expectations, and meaningful participation). To a far greater degree than students at other Oakland high schools, they agreed that "teachers show how classroom lessons are helpful to me in real life," and they reported strong academic support at a higher rate than their Oakland peers did. Edging out their counterparts, 73 percent of the Oakland International sample said they planned to go on to a two- or four-year college or university. And far more reported that they had a mentor at school who advised them on their postsecondary planning. (Interestingly, more than half said that their schoolwork had inspired them to pursue a career in math, science, engineering, or technology.)

Students also rated the social and emotional aspects of their school higher than did peers districtwide. Their perception that "adults at this school treat all students with respect" was extremely high (nearly doubling the district average). They had greater confidence than their peers that conflicts would result in a safe and confidential resolution process. And they also considered themselves involved in school leadership at a higher rate.

An Unstoppable Momentum

When Oakland International students describe their pasts and their futures, one hears them creating narratives with an intergenerational frame that is larger than themselves. They are coming to see setbacks not as the end of the story but as obstacles from which they and their families are bouncing back. Such "sense-making" narratives contribute mightily to resilience, psychologists have found.[8] And as these adolescents integrate the perspectives of others into their immigration stories, their own understanding of their emerging identity increases and their voices grow more confident.[9]

In his native Guatemala, Amilanu said, he saw a lot of racism. "They used to call me 'monkey' because I'm Mayan; they said I didn't belong to their civilization." But at Oakland International, "they taught me that it's different," he said. "We have to live together, we have to bring unity between everyone." After earning his law degree someday, he wants to return to his country and help Mayan people fight for their rights. "If I could, I would do something good for this country, too . . . maybe come back to Oakland and work in this school to help other kids like people helped me."

"In the future I want to be a software engineer," said Régis, who found his sense of belonging on the soccer fields here. "That's why I'm training in computer class to understand what computer is the best, so when I go to college I'll be ready." Kamilah, who hopes to become a midwife, is trying to arrange her senior internship in that field. Zelia wants to go to "the best four-year college that would have me" and to have a career in accounting. Pedro, who acted out his fears in his first year at the school, now plans to go into business or perhaps become a chef.

On the wall of Jennifer Kelly-DeWitt's classroom, her advisory students have posted their aspirations in large letters on bright paper. Beneath Aye's name it says: "I will go to college. I will be a doctor. I will help my people. I will take care my family." Zahraa wrote: "I will be a mom. I will be an engineer. I will read 100 books." Small mistakes may show up here and there, but the conviction of their words carries a momentum that seems unstoppable.

CHAPTER 7

From Practice to Policy

A Call to Action

T HE PORTRAITS IN THIS BOOK show that social and emotional learning *can* be integrated into the day-to-day life of public high schools, with remarkable results. When compared with schools with similar demographics, our four schools that built social and emotional learning into their original design have consistently produced stand-out academic results: strong attendance and low dropout rates, good proficiency results on state assessments, and a high percentage of students going on to college. After social and emotional learning became Fenger's driving force, its academic results made it one of the most improved high schools in Chicago.

Other benefits of social and emotional learning mattered almost as much as test scores to these stakeholders. With adolescents who struggled to find their stride, such learning developed confidence and maturity. For youth haunted by brokenness and violence, it offered a lifeline.

At a moment when civic engagement and thoughtful discourse seem more precious than ever, these schools demonstrate the viability of communities of respect, where diversity is valued and everyone participates. As the students say at Springfield Renaissance, "We are crew, not passengers."

We have also identified the critical elements—from a web of structural supports to a curriculum of connection and engagement—that provided the backbone for these schools' successful efforts. School leaders and staff called on a multitude of effective practices to bring these elements to life: daily advisories, student choice, mental health triage, growth mind-set building, interactions conveying that each student matters. All adolescent learners benefit from developing a sense of agency as scholars and budding adults. But these exemplars underline the special potency of these practices in a context where students live with inequities that constrict their futures.

The big question is not "Does social-emotional learning work?" Given the evidence, we must ask why more high schools do not put it at the very core of what they do. In these last pages, we examine some of the challenges and opportunities that question raises—and their implications for policy.

To start, we need new language that ends the "versus" between cognitive and noncognitive factors in discussions of learning and mastery. As education scholar Mike Rose urges, we must reclaim the full meaning of cognition: "robust and intellectual, intimately connected to character and social development, and directed toward the creation of a better world."[1] Science has clearly established that academic, social, and emotional learning *are* deeply mutual. School leaders and policy makers must create time and supports in the school day to bring all those essential dimensions to bear on student success.

In turn, we need learning standards that treat SEL as integral to the curriculum. Common Core standards already require students to collaborate, to consider the perspectives of others, and to persevere in solving problems. Such competencies already have gained a constituency that pushes for high school graduates to demonstrate "twenty-first century skills." A 2013 survey of 605 teachers found that more than 75 percent believed that a greater focus on social and emotional learning would be a "major benefit" to students because of its positive impact on "workforce readiness, school attendance and graduation, life success, college preparation and academic success."[2] The Illinois Learning Standards now include social and emotional development standards.[3] At the time of this writing, legislators in California and Washington were working on bills that would recommend statewide standards for SEL.

Taking stock of student gains with regard to SEL presents a complex challenge and supplies yet another argument for assessments to include performance-based measures. As with student drivers, the written test reveals less than the road test. Does the learner actually persevere, for example, when the going gets tough? Known for a focus on character building, schools in the national Knowledge Is Power Program (KIPP) charter network award students scores for character growth as well as academics. Advocates foresee a day when a student's "CPA" would matter as much as the GPA.

Our investigation also highlights important structures and practices in high schools that foster strong student–teacher relationships and a culture of respectful, intentional, and inclusive community. Discrete, evidence-based SEL programs such as those catalogued by CASEL play a critical part in that ecology. But their potential is increased, we have found, when integrated into daily instruction in a systemic approach.

As we have demonstrated throughout this book, the convergence of academic, social, and emotional learning serves *all* students well. It misses the point to embrace SEL largely as a behavior-management or character-development tool for at-risk students in urban schools, though certainly such programs play a part in closing the achievement gap. Our five study schools demonstrate the capacity of SEL to enrich student learning, aspiration, and engagement across the entire spectrum of students.

We applaud the rising interest in restorative justice programs as an alternative to harmful zero tolerance policies. The evidence is irrefutable: harsh and exclusionary disciplinary procedures have helped feed a school-to-prison pipeline, disproportionately filled with students of color and those with a history of abuse, neglect, poverty, or learning disabilities.[4] Restorative practices have proven themselves more positive, effective, and just. Replacing zero tolerance with alternatives like those found in these schools offers second chances: for students struggling to find their footing in school and for teachers struggling to address the needs of their most difficult students.

Sadly, the youth in question sometimes need much more than the chance to right their wrongs and stay in school, however critical these are. They may need help managing the chronic stressors that lie behind their defiance—worries linked to family, health (mental and physical), safety, and sometimes food and shelter too.

Though cognizant of the limits of what schools can do, we know the exorbitant costs of the consequences of neglect and school failure. The annual cost of keeping one adjudicated youth at the Cook County Juvenile Detention Center in Chicago currently exceeds $200,000, by some estimates.[5] The three-year federal school improvement grant at Fenger High School—which underwrote the SEL supports and additional staff that fueled the school's turnaround—cost roughly $3,000 per student per year. Now that grant has expired and the extra staff has gone, but the stressors in those students' lives will continue. (Researchers at Columbia University recently examined the economic returns from investments in six prominent social and emotional interventions and found that, on average, "for every dollar invested, there was a return of more than eleven dollars."[6])

We see occasions for hope in schools that forge substantial partnerships with community-based organizations to provide social and mental health supports for students. And we are encouraged by national initiatives like My Brother's Keeper, with its promise of building "ladders of opportunity and unlocking the full potential of our young people, including boys and young men of color." But these efforts do not match the intensive, day-to-day investment that students at Fenger High received when the money (almost) met the need.

Finally—though perhaps first of all—teacher preparation programs must equip new teachers with the core competencies necessary to foster social and emotional learning. They will need guidance in creating the safe, respectful, motivating, and engaging classrooms that develop minds and character equally. They will need coaching to help their students stand in the shoes of others (and grow into bigger shoes, too). Experienced guides and mentors can model the social and emotional skills that novice teachers will soon be modeling for their own students. In spring of 2015, several bills were introduced in Congress that would allow federal grants to be used for training teachers in social and emotional learning programs.

Such shifts in policy can provide the crucial supports that would extend and lend leverage to the exemplars we have presented in this volume. We offer these five portraits not merely as inspiration, but as proof points of the power and sustainability of social and emotional learning in our nation's secondary schools. We hope that readers will take these vibrant journeys toward excellence into their own hearts and minds, and will hear them, above all, as a clarion call to action.

Notes

CHAPTER 1

1. Goleman, D. (1995). *Emotional intelligence: Why it can matter more than IQ*. New York: Random House, Bantam Books.
2. Durlak, J., Weissberg, R., Dymnicki A., Taylor R., & Schellinger K. (2011). The impact of enhancing students' social and emotional learning: A meta-analysis of school-based universal interventions. *Child Development, 82,* 1, 405–432.
3. Toshalis, E., & Nakkula, M. J. (2012). Motivation, engagement, and student voice. Boston, MA: Jobs for the Future: Students at the Center.
4. Farrington, C. A., et al. (2012). *Teaching adolescents to become learners: The role of noncognitive factors in shaping school performance*. Chicago: Consortium on Chicago School Research at the University of Chicago.
5. Conley, D. (2013, January 23). Rethinking the notion of "noncognitive." *Education Week*. Retrieved from http://www.edweek.org/ew/articles/2013/01/23/18conley.h32.html.
6. Rose, M. (2013, January 15). Giving cognition a bad name. *Education Week*. Retrieved from http://www.edweek.org/ew/articles/2013/01/16/17rose_ep.h32.html
7. Dweck, C. (2006). *Mindset: The new psychology of success*. New York: Random House.
8. Tough, P. (2012). *How children succeed: Grit, curiosity, and the hidden power of character*. Boston: Houghton Mifflin; see also Duckworth, A., et al. (2007). Grit: Perseverance and passion for long-term goals. *Journal of Personality and Social Psychology, 92,* 1087–1101.

CHAPTER 2

1. Among the most influential of these were the following: U.S. Department of Education (1983). *A nation at risk*. Washington, DC: National Commission on Excellence in Education; Boyer, E. L. (1983). *High school: A report on secondary education in America* (a report for the Carnegie Foundation

for the Advancement of Teaching). New York: Harper & Row; Sizer, T. R. (1984). *Horace's compromise: The dilemma of the American high school.* Boston: Houghton Mifflin; Powell, A. G., Farrar, E., & Cohen, D. K. (1985). *The shopping mall high school: Winners and losers in the educational marketplace.* Boston: Houghton Mifflin; and Hampel, R. L. (1986). *The last little citadel: American high schools since 1940.* Boston: Houghton Mifflin.

2. Full details appear in Bloom, H. S., & Unterman, R. (2013, August). *Sustained progress: New findings about the effectiveness and operation of small public high schools of choice in New York City.* New York: MDRC. East Side Community's middle and high schools have consistently received grades of A on the New York Department of Education's school report cards.

3. Roderick, M. R., et al. (2008). *From high school to the future: Potholes on the road to college.* Chicago: Consortium on Chicago School Research at University of Chicago.

4. Details of developing the "100 percent respect" campaign at ESCS appear in Guldin, M. (2009). Please respect me! *Principal Leadership, 9*(5), 24–27; and at http://www.100respect.com.

5. Farrington, C. A., et al. (2012). *Teaching adolescents to become learners: The role of noncognitive factors in shaping school performance: A critical literature review.* Chicago: Consortium on Chicago School Research at the University of Chicago.

6. See, for example, Oran, G. (2009). Culturally responsive pedagogy. Retrieved from Education.com; Jackson, A. W., & Davis, G. (2000). *Turning Points 2000: Educating adolescents in the 21st century.* New York: Carnegie Corporation; Phinney, J. (1989). Stages of ethnic identity development in minority group adolescents. *Journal of Early Adolescence, 9,* 1–2, 34–49.

7. Booth, D. W., & Rowsell, J. (2007). *The literacy principal: Leading, supporting and assessing reading and writing initiatives* (2nd ed.). Markham, Ont.: Pembroke Publishers.

8. Francois, C. (2012). Getting at the core of literacy improvement: A case study of an urban secondary school. *Education and Urban Society.* Advance online publication. doi: 10.1177/0013124512458116; and Francois, C. (2013). Reading in the crawl space: A study of an urban school's literacy-focused community of practice. *Teachers College Record, 115*(5), 1–35. www.tcrecord.org, ID: 16966.

9. New York Performance Standards Consortium. (2013). *Educating for the 21st century: Data report on the New York Performance Standards Consortium.* New York: Performance Standards Consortium. Retrieved from http://performanceassessment.org/articles/DataReport_ NY_PSC.pdf.

10. Lazar, S. (2011, January 28). Authentic accountability: Roundtable portfolio presentations. *New York: Gotham News.* Retrieved from http://gothamschools .org/2011/01/28/authentic-accountability-roundtable-portfolio-presentations/.

CHAPTER 3

1. See Sergiovanni, T. (1993, April). *Organizations or communities? Changing the metaphor changes the theory.* Paper presented to the American Educational Research Association, Atlanta, GA.
2. See Osterman, K. F. (2000). Students' need for belonging in the school community. *Review of Educational Research, 70*(3), 323–367.
3. See Farrington, C. A. (2013). *Academic mindsets as a critical component of deeper learning.* A white paper prepared for the William and Flora Hewlett Foundation, p. 5.
4. See Scales, P. C., & Benson, P. L. (2005). Prosocial orientation and community service. In K. A. Moore & L. Lippman (Eds.), *What do children need to flourish?* (pp. 339–356). New York: Springer; Scales, P. C., & Roehlkepartain, E. C. (2004). Service to others: A "gateway asset" for school success and healthy development. In J. Kielsmeier, M. Neal, & M. McKinnon (Eds.) *Growing to greatness 2004: The state of service-learning in the United States* (pp. 26–32). St. Paul, MN: National Youth Leadership Council.
5. See Search Institute. (2007). 40 developmental assets for adolescents. Retrieved from http://bit.ly/1mUZVGw.
6. See Stipek, D. (2006). Relationships matter. *Educational Leadership, 64*(1), 46–49 ; Bryk, A., & Schneider, B. (2002). *Trust in schools: A core resource for improvement.* New York, NY: Russell Sage Foundation; Cornelius-White, J. (2007). Learner-centered teacher-student relationships are effective: A meta-analysis. *Review of Educational Research, 77*(1), 113–143; Rhonda, D. L. (2011). The influence of affective teacher–student relationships on students' school engagement and achievement: A meta-analytic approach. *Review of Educational Research, 81*, 493–529.
7. See Farrington, C. A., et al. (2012). *Teaching adolescents to become learners: The role of noncognitive factors in shaping school performance: A critical literature review.* Chicago: Consortium on Chicago School Research at the University of Chicago, p. 2.
8. See Farrington, C. A. (2013). *Academic mindsets as a critical component of deeper learning.* A white paper prepared for the William and Flora Hewlett Foundation.
9. Goleman, D. (1995). *Emotional intelligence: Why it can matter more than IQ.* New York: Random House, Bantam Books.

CHAPTER 4

1. Belonging to Expeditionary Learning also lent gravitas to the new school from the funding perspective. From 2005 to 2008, the initial grant from the Bill & Melinda Gates Foundation made possible the design and launch stages

of Springfield Renaissance, including substantial professional development for its early cohorts of teachers. More funding came from a three-year federal magnet school grant for 2007–2010. As the school built its reputation, it won a 2010 Catalyst for Change award and grant from the Nellie Mae Education Foundation, followed by a $50,000 Commonwealth Innovation School grant in 2011 from the Massachusetts Department of Education. No grant money came with the school's designation as a Magnet School of Excellence in 2011 and 2013, by Magnet Schools of America. As of the end of the 2011–2012 school year, Renaissance was working within its regular school budget.

2. Blackwell, L. S., Trzesniewski, K. H., & Dweck, C. S. (2007). Implicit theories of intelligence predict achievement across an adolescent transition: A longitudinal study and an intervention. *Child Development, 78*, 246–263.

3. For a summary, see Osterman, K. F. (2000). Students' need for belonging in the school community. *Review of Educational Research, 70*(3), 323–367.

4. See, for example, Deci, E., Vallerand, R., Pelletier, L., & Ryan, R. (1991). Motivation and education: The self-determination perspective. *Educational Psychologist, 26*, 325–346.

5. Rothstein, R. (2014, April 17). *Brown v. Board at 60: Why have we been so disappointed? What have we learned?* Washington, DC: Economic Policy Institute.

6. Schwartz, H. (2010, October 15). *Housing policy is school policy: Economically integrative housing promotes academic success in Montgomery County, Maryland.* Washington, DC: The Century Foundation; Johnson, R. C. (2001, January). *Long-run impacts of school desegregation and school quality on adult attainments.* National Bureau of Economic Research Working Paper 16664 (revised, May 2014).

7. See Halpern, R., Heckman, P., & Larson, R. (2013). *Realizing the potential of learning in middle adolescence.* Quincy, MA: Nellie Mae Education Foundation.

CHAPTER 5

1. Bristol, T. (2013, September 4). Calling black men to the blackboard [Web log post]. Albert Shanker Institute Blog. Retrieved from http://bit.ly/1xy6Xko

2. Christians, T. (2012, November 6). One key to education reform [Web log post]. UMOJA blog. Retrieved from http://bit.ly/1FbS2uA

3. For nearly a century, Boys Town in Omaha, Nebraska, has given at-risk children the family, support, and care they need to overcome their circumstances and realize their potential. It produces books and educational materials, runs a hotline, offers educational training for schools, and provides direct services to children and families through ten locations nationwide. Boys Town began

as a home for underprivileged and delinquent boys, memorialized in the 1938 film *Boys Town* starring Spencer Tracy.

4. Response to Intervention (RTI) aims to integrate assessment and intervention within a multilevel prevention system to increase student achievement and reduce behavioral problems. With RTI, schools use data to identify students at risk for poor learning outcomes, monitor student progress, provide evidence-based interventions, and adjust the intensity and nature of those interventions depending on a student's responsiveness. There are two frameworks: one for academics and another for behavior. Both include three tiers: Tier I interventions address the needs of all students; Tier II provides targeted group interventions for at-risk students; and Tier III involves intensive individual interventions for the highest-risk students. Research points to both the promise and complexities of RTI. See http://www.rti4success.org/ and http://www.rtinetwork.org/.

5. Instituted largely as a reaction to the 1999 Columbine school shooting in Colorado, zero tolerance policies remove situational discretion from school officials and institute mandated minimum penalties that often include police involvement for drug, weapon, and violence offenses on school grounds and trigger automatic suspension or expulsion.

   While one cannot accurately measure the full scope of zero tolerance policies—some are written into state legislatures, others implemented at the school district level by local school boards—statistics from many states show these policies disproportionately harm students of color and produce a "school-to-prison pipeline."

   A 2008 review of the research on zero tolerance policies, by the American Psychological Association, found little evidence that they produced safer schools. "Clearly, an alternative course is necessary," the APA task force concluded, "that can guarantee safe school environments without removing large numbers of students from the opportunity to learn." See http://www.apa.org/pubs/info/reports/zero-tolerance.pdf.

6. Tough, P. (2012). *How children succeed: Grit, curiosity, and the hidden power of character*. New York: Random House, 1–2, 4–7, 194.

7. In 2004, the Chicago Public Schools adopted a social-emotional policy that, among other things, required all schools to develop screening, early intervention, and clinical referral. In 2008, Chicago's Office of School Improvement (OSI) adopted the CARE team model to help the policy in practice. CARE teams are school-based groups composed of school counselors, school social workers, school psychologists, community mental health providers, and administrators to collaborate in finding solutions to the problems of at-risk students and families; deliver three levels of interventions that address students' social, emotional, and behavioral needs; facilitate referrals to further support student needs; work closely with school personnel (e.g., teachers,

deans, student advocates) and community-based organizations; and gather and analyze data to track and improve their services.

8. Center on the Developing Child. (2011). Toxic stress derails healthy development [video file]. Harvard University. Retrieved from http://bit.ly/1BB6Gwi

9. Developed by two psychologists in 1989, the Think First anger management curriculum targets high school students, age thirteen to eighteen, whose relationships with peers or adults are conflict-ridden. It aims to equip these students with the social processing and behavioral skills needed to reduce impulsive and aggressive responses to anger. Think First groups meet for fifteen sessions. Essential components include role-plays, discussions, weekly goal setting, and self-monitoring.

10. Created in 1999 by a team of researchers and psychologists in Los Angeles, Cognitive Behavioral Intervention for Trauma in Schools (CBITS) was designed for children who go to school weighed down by some form of violence, trauma, or maltreatment and suffer post-traumatic stress syndrome. CBITS provides mental health screening and a cognitive-behavioral approach aimed at reducing PTSD symptoms and enhancing the child's ability to handle future stresses. The program consists of ten group sessions, one to three individual sessions, two parent sessions, and one teacher individual session. Several national agencies that assess the quality of mental health interventions cite CBITS as a recommended program. See http://www.cbitsprogram.org/.

11. Fink, J. W. L. (2014). Building a positive school culture: How one school transformed from violence to haven [Web log post]. We Are Teachers. Retrieved from http://bit.ly/1kxgwBC

12. Allensworth, E. M., & Easton, J. Q. (2005, June). *The on-track indicator as a predictor of high school graduation*. With commentary by D. Chaplin. Chicago: Consortium on Chicago School Research at the University of Chicago.

13. Balfanz, R., & Byrnes, V. (2012). The importance of being in school: A report on absenteeism in the nation's schools. In R. Balfanz & V. Byrnes (Eds.), *Chronic absenteeism: Summarizing what we know from nationally available data* (pp. 1–4). Baltimore: Johns Hopkins University Center for Social Organization of Schools.

14. Kutash, J., et al., (2010, September). *The school turnaround field guide*. Boston, MA: FSG Social Impact Advisers.

15. Warn, D. (2014, August 14). Prevent summer melt and keep students enrolled in college. fosterEDU. Retrieved from http://bit.ly/1tDH4DO.

CHAPTER 6

1. Community partners include Refugee Transitions, Soccer Without Borders, Asian Community Mental Health Services, East Bay Asian Youth Center (EBAYC), Lincoln Child Center, OTX West, the 180 Degrees Program, Parent

Leadership and Action Network, the OUSD Refugee and Asylee Student Assistance Program, the Association for Continuing Education, University of California Berkeley ACES Program, Project Peace East Bay, First Presbyterian Church of Berkeley, Community Health for Asian Americans, the OUSD TUPE program, and the University of California Berkeley School of Social Work.

2. Research in the science of learning increasingly recognizes the close interdependence of physical and intellectual well-being and the close interplay of the emotional and cognitive. See, for example, Immordino-Yang, M. H., & Damasio, A. R. (2007). We feel, therefore we learn: The relevance of affective and social neuroscience to education. *Mind, Brain and Education, 1*(1), 3–10; and Huppert, F. A. (2005). Positive emotions and cognition: Developmental, neuroscience and health perspectives. In J. P. Forgas (Ed.), *Hearts and minds: Affective influences on social cognition and behavior* (Frontiers of Social Psychology Series, pp. 237–239). New York: Psychology Press.

3. For a review of this research, see Nilsson, L. G. (2000). Remembering actions and words. In E. Tulving & F. I. M. Craik (Eds.), *The Oxford handbook of memory* (pp. 137–148). New York: Oxford University Press.

4. Glenberg, A.M., & Kaschak, M.P. (2002). Grounding language in action. *Psychonomic Bulletin & Review, 9,* 558–565.

5. Eisner, E. (2002). *The arts and the creation of mind.* New Haven, CT: Yale University Press.

6. Perkins, D. N., Jay, E., & Tishman, S. (1993). Beyond abilities: A dispositional theory of thinking. *Merrill-Palmer Quarterly, 39*(1), 1–21.

7. Hetland, L., Winner, E., Veenema, S., & Sheridan, K. M. (2007). *Studio thinking: The real benefits of visual arts education.* New York: Teachers College Press.

8. See Fivush, R., Duke, M., & Bohanek, J. G. (2010, February 23). "Do you know . . .": The power of family history in adolescent identity and well-being. *Journal of Family Life,* http://publichistorycommons.org/wp-content/uploads/2013/12/The-power-of-family-history-in-adolescent-identity.pdf; and Habermas, T., & Bluck, S. (2000), Getting a life: The emergence of the life story in adolescence. *Psychological Bulletin, 126,* 748–769.

9. Fivush, R., Habermas, T., Waters, T. E. A., & Zaman, W. (2011, October). The making of autobiographical memory: Intersections of culture, narratives and identity. *International Journal of Psychology, 46*(5), 321–345.

CHAPTER 7

1. Rose, M. (2013, January 15). Giving cognition a bad name. *Education Week.* Retrieved from http://www.edweek.org/ew/articles/2013/01/16/17rose_ep.h32.html

2. Bridgeland, J., Bruce, M., & Hariharan, A., with Peter D. Hart Research Associates. (2013). *The missing piece: A national teacher survey on how social and emotional learning can empower children and transform schools*. Washington, DC: Civic Enterprises.

3. Illinois State Board of Education. (2015). Illinois Learning Standards and Social-Emotional Learning. Retrieved from http://www.isbe.net/ils/

4. See, for example, PBS. (2013, March 28). How bad is the school-to-prison pipeline: Facts. Retrieved from http://to.pbs.org/1ebSc50

5. Chicago Youth Justice Data Project. (2014, April). The conscious Chicagoan's guide to youth incarceration and retention. Retrieved from http://bit.ly/1EnKwf5

6. Shriver, T., & Bridgeland, J. (2015, February 26). Social and emotional learning pays off. *Education Week*. Retrieved from http://bit.ly/1aCEVoQ

Acknowledgments

W E OWE OUR DEEPEST GRATITUDE to the teachers, school leaders, and students whose voices fill the pages that follow. Honest and trusting, they shared their experiences, wisdom, and time with us at every turn, eager to move social and emotional learning to center stage in the public discourse about what helps students succeed. These educators and youth have shaped remarkable schools from their shared visions, purposeful community, and tireless work. Each of them deserves acknowledgment, although space will not allow that here. Instead, we name the principals who led their efforts at the time of our research: Mark Federman, at East Side Community School in New York City; Ginger Noyes, at Quest Early College High School outside Houston; Stephen Mahoney, at Springfield Renaissance School in Massachusetts; Elizabeth Dozier, at Fenger High School in Chicago; and Carmelita Reyes and Sailaja Suresh, at Oakland International High School in California.

With its genuine curiosity about social and emotional learning in secondary schools and its generous support for our research and documentation, the NoVo Foundation put wind in our sails throughout this project. The wise questions and counsel of Nancy Walser, our editor at Harvard Education Press, helped shape our narratives; and her colleagues in design, production, and marketing made their own essential contributions. We thank all these good people—as well as you, gentle readers—for helping bring our accounts to public attention. May the influence of these five schools extend to students everywhere.

—Barbara Cervone and Kathleen Cushman

About the Authors

Barbara Cervone, EdD (HUGSE), is founder and president of What Kids Can Do, Inc., an international nonprofit organization that promotes the value of young people tackling projects that combine powerful learning with public purpose. From 1994 to 2001 she directed Walter H. Annenberg's "Challenge to the Nation," then the largest private investment in public education in the nation's history. In 2008 Dr. Cervone was awarded the Purpose Prize. Her many publications include "Powerful Learning with Public Purpose," in *New Directions for Youth Development* (Jossey-Bass, 2010); *In Our Village*, a book series documenting youth perspectives in international settings (Next Generation Press); and the first chapter, "Learning from the Leaders: Core Practices of Six Schools," in *Anytime, Anywhere: Student-Centered Learning for Schools and Teachers* (Harvard Education Press, 2013).

Kathleen Cushman is an educator and writer who has specialized in the lives and learning of youth for twenty-five years. From 1989 to 2001 she documented theory and practice in schools nationwide for the Coalition of Essential Schools and the Annenberg Challenge, publishing many books, including *Schooling and the Real World* (Jossey-Bass, 1999) and *The Collected Horace* (Coalition of Essential Schools, 2001). In 2001 Cushman cofounded What Kids Can Do, Inc., with Barbara Cervone. Her work there has resulted in ten books, including the best-selling *Fires in the Bathroom* series (New Press, 2003, 2006), *Fires in the Mind: What Kids Can Tell Us About Motivation and Mastery* (Jossey-Bass, 2010), and *The Motivation Equation* (Next Generation Press, 2013). Her articles regularly appear in *Educational Leadership, Phi Delta Kappan*, and other periodicals and blogs for educators.

Index